DATE			

DISEASES & DISORDERS

Waterborne Illnesses

Peggy J. Parks

LUCENT BOOKS

A part of Gale, Cengage Learning

CENGAGE Learning·

Detroit • New York • San Francisco • New Haven, Conn • Waterville, Maine • London

LIBRARY OF CONGRESS CATALOGING-IN-PUBLICATION DATA

Parks, Peggy J., 1951-
  Waterborne illnesses / by Peggy J. Parks.
    pages cm. -- (Diseases & disorders)
  Includes bibliographical references and index.
  ISBN 978-1-4205-0935-9 (hardcover)
  1. Waterborne infection. 2. Waterborne infection--Prevention--International cooperation. 3. Water--Pollution--Health aspects. I. Title.
  RA642.W3P38 2013
  613.6'2--dc23
                                                    2012047509

Lucent Books
27500 Drake Rd.
Farmington Hills, MI 48331

ISBN-13: 978-1-4205-0935-9
ISBN-10: 1-4205-0935-7

Printed in the United States of America
2 3 4 5 6 7 17 16 15 14 13

Table of Contents

"The Most Difficult Puzzles Ever Devised"

Charles Best, one of the pioneers in the search for a cure for diabetes, once explained what it is about medical research that intrigued him so. "It's not just the gratification of knowing one is helping people," he confided, "although that probably is a more heroic and selfless motivation. Those feelings may enter in, but truly, what I find best is the feeling of going toe to toe with nature, of trying to solve the most difficult puzzles ever devised. The answers are there somewhere, those keys that will solve the puzzle and make the patient well. But how will those keys be found?"

Since the dawn of civilization, nothing has so puzzled people—and often frightened them, as well—as the onset of illness in a body or mind that had seemed healthy before. A seizure, the inability of a heart to pump, the sudden deterioration of muscle tone in a small child—being unable to reverse such conditions or even to understand why they occur was unspeakably frustrating to healers. Even before there were names for such conditions, even before they were understood at all, each was a reminder of how complex the human body was, and how vulnerable.

While our grappling with understanding diseases has been frustrating at times, it has also provided some of humankind's most heroic accomplishments. Alexander Fleming's accidental discovery in 1928 of a mold that could be turned into penicillin has resulted in the saving of untold millions of lives. The isolation of the enzyme insulin has reversed what was once a death sentence for anyone with diabetes. There have been great strides in combating conditions for which there is not yet a cure, too. Medicines can help AIDS patients live longer, diagnostic tools such as mammography and ultrasounds can help doctors find tumors while they are treatable, and laser surgery techniques have made the most intricate, minute operations routine.

This "toe-to-toe" competition with diseases and disorders is even more remarkable when seen in a historical continuum. An astonishing amount of progress has been made in a very short time. Just two hundred years ago, the existence of germs as a cause of some diseases was unknown. In fact, it was less than 150 years ago that a British surgeon named Joseph Lister had difficulty persuading his fellow doctors that washing their hands before delivering a baby might increase the chances of a healthy delivery (especially if they had just attended to a diseased patient)!

Each book in Lucent's Diseases and Disorders series explores a disease or disorder and the knowledge that has been accumulated (or discarded) by doctors through the years. Each book also examines the tools used for pinpointing a diagnosis, as well as the various means that are used to treat or cure a disease. Finally, new ideas are presented—techniques or medicines that may be on the horizon.

Frustration and disappointment are still part of medicine, for not every disease or condition can be cured or prevented. But the limitations of knowledge are being pushed outward constantly; the "most difficult puzzles ever devised" are finding challengers every day.

When Water Sickens and Kills

On March 22, 2010, United Nations secretary-general Ban Ki-moon issued a statement to commemorate World Water Day. He began by acknowledging how precious a resource water is: "Water is the source of life and the link that binds all living beings on the planet." Water is indeed essential, because every form of life on earth depends on it for survival—but the world's supply of freshwater is in peril. Much of it has become dangerously polluted, which has led to a global epidemic of waterborne illness. In his statement, Ban made it clear that the responsibility for this pollution rests with humans. "Day after day," he said, "we pour millions of tons of untreated sewage and industrial and agricultural waste into the world's water systems. Clean water has become scarce." Ban then shared a dismal statistic: More people die from unsafe water than from all types of violence, including war. "These deaths," he said, "are an affront to our common humanity."[1]

Countries in Crisis

The number of deaths from waterborne illness is truly staggering. According to the World Health Organization (WHO), more than 3 million people die every year from these illnesses, and tens of millions more are sickened. Because young children's immune systems are still developing, they are especially vulnerable to infection and disease and are the most likely to develop waterborne illnesses—and the most likely to die from them. An investigation commissioned by the United Nations found that four thousand children die every day from diseases caused by ingesting filthy, contaminated water.

A United Nations investigation found that nearly four thousand children die every day from ingesting contaminated water. Here, residents of a village in Burkina Faso try their hardest to get water from a drying-up well.

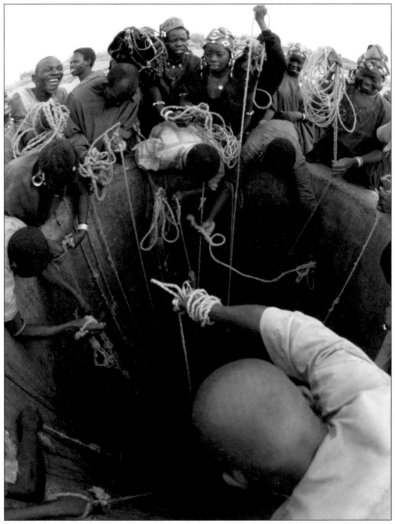

By far the greatest prevalence of waterborne illness is in developing countries, those that struggle with extreme poverty, government instability, and poor human health. The WHO states that nearly 800 million people in the developing world have no access to clean, safe drinking water (also called potable water), and billions lack even the most basic sanitation facilities. One developing country that is known for severe water shortages and widespread contamination of rivers, lakes, and streams, is India. A United Nations evaluation of water resources in 122 countries worldwide ranked India 120th for its water quality, and other studies have shown that at least 70 percent of India's water supply is seriously polluted with sewage. As a result, waterborne illnesses are rampant. In June 2012 an outbreak of the waterborne illness hepatitis E struck the Indian city of Ichalkaranji. State health officials determined that leaks from sewage pipes had contaminated the Panchganga River, which is the main source of drinking water for residents of the city. By the time the outbreak was under control, more than four thousand people had fallen ill, and at least eighteen of them had died.

America Struggles, Too

Such serious outbreaks are rare in industrialized countries, but that does not mean these countries are unaffected by waterborne illness. A number of these illnesses are prevalent throughout the world, even in countries with modern systems for sanitation and water treatment. This is true in the United States, which is known for having some of the world's safest drinking water. Since the water is heavily regulated by the U.S. Environmental Protection Agency (EPA), it is considered to be free of dangerous contaminants—but that is true only for cities, not rural areas. According to the Centers for Disease Control and Prevention (CDC), at least 15 percent of the U.S. population is not served by municipal water systems. The CDC writes: "Instead, they use individual wells and very small drinking water systems not covered by the Safe Water Drinking Act; these wells and systems are often untested and contaminated."[2] Because this water is not subject to federal regulation, it carries a high risk for waterborne illness.

Another source of waterborne illness in the United States is recreational water, which includes bodies of freshwater such as lakes, rivers, and ponds where people swim and play. A CDC report published in September 2011 showed that the number of disease outbreaks related to swimming in recreational water has steadily increased over the years, rising 72 percent since 2005. Studies by the Natural Resources Defense Council have found that more than 3 million Americans become sick each year from contact with raw sewage that has overflowed from sanitary sewers into recreational waters during heavy rainstorms. This can wash numerous contaminants into the water, such as *Escherichia coli* (E. coli), a group of bacteria in the coliform family that is associated with intestinal illness. Most types of E. coli live in the intestinal tracts of humans and other mammals and are harmless, but others are toxic enough to cause serious disease, brain damage, and even death.

A Formidable Problem

It is a disturbing reality that wherever water is found, there is potential for waterborne illness. These illnesses exist everywhere, although the worst problems are in developing countries that continuously struggle with shortages of clean water for drinking, bathing, and cooking. Scientists and health officials continue to study this issue and work toward improving water supplies and sanitation practices throughout the world. Although it will take years to accomplish, their efforts, along with those of humanitarian workers, may someday reduce the incidence of waterborne illness and perhaps eradicate it altogether.

CHAPTER ONE

What Are Waterborne Illnesses?

Years of scientific research have shown a clear link between disease and contaminated water. As a result, it is now an undisputed fact that the water people depend on for survival can also make them sick. There was a time, however, when this connection was not known. Prior to the nineteenth century, scientists scoffed at the notion that disease-causing organisms lived and thrived in water. The prevailing belief was that all diseases were caused by miasma, or toxic vapors in the air. The first person to prove this theory wrong was British physician John Snow. During the mid-1850s Snow studied an epidemic of the deadly illness known as cholera, which was rampant in London, England. By investigating the way the disease was spread, Snow demonstrated that cholera was caused by infectious bacteria in water, rather than by bad air. He could not identify the specific bacterium, so he referred to it as "cholera poison."

German scientist Robert Koch provided the missing link several decades later while working in Calcutta, India. He examined samples of river water under a microscope and observed a comma-shaped bacterium that is now known as *Vibrio cholerae*. When examining stool samples from cholera patients, Koch saw the same organism—which proved the connection between the bacteria and the disease. His theory was further strengthened when the bacteria were not present in stool samples from healthy people. Koch's findings, along with Snow's, laid the groundwork for research on other illnesses. Like cholera, many of these illnesses were found to be waterborne.

German doctor Robert Koch made the connection between bacteria in foul water and cholera outbreaks. He laid the foundation for investigations into other waterborne illnesses.

Pathogenic Bacteria and Viruses

Organisms such as bacteria that are capable of causing disease are known as pathogens and are said to be pathogenic. Most types (scientists call them strains) of bacteria are not pathogenic. They exist naturally in air, water, soil, plants, and the bodies of humans and other animals. These one-celled organisms are so tiny that a million could fit on the head of a pin, and they have the ability to divide and multiply on their own. In humans bacteria perform essential functions like fighting off infection and helping produce vitamins that are needed for good health.

Bacteria can also aid with digestion, which is the case with most strains of E. coli. These bacteria live and grow in the intestines of warm-blooded creatures to help the body break down food into digestible sugars or proteins. But a few strains of E. coli have undergone genetic changes that have made them pathogenic. Once a human or animal is infected with these E. coli pathogens, as the American Academy of Microbiology explains, "the bacteria will be shed in manure or feces."[3] When water is contaminated by this waste matter, such as from sewage overflows or manure from infected farm animals, the water can make people sick.

Like E. coli and other strains of pathogenic bacteria, viruses can be transmitted by contaminated water. Viruses, however, are different from bacteria in several ways. They are tinier than even the smallest bacteria and are not naturally present in the human body. Viruses are also not capable of growing and multiplying on their own. Instead, they must seek out the body of an animal or human (known as a host) and attack living cells that will enable them to reproduce. When someone is infected by a virus, the virus breaks into the body's cells and takes control, instructing the cells to manufacture the parts it needs to make more viral particles. In the process the cells burst open and are destroyed, which causes the virus to spread throughout the body.

Parasitic Pathogens

In addition to bacteria and viruses, another type of disease-causing pathogen is the parasite. It is even more reliant on

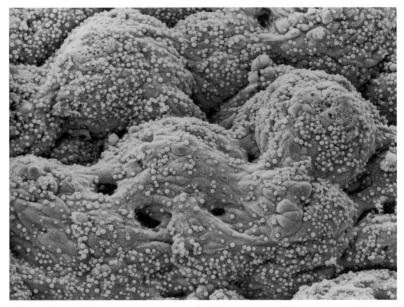

This colored electron micrograph shows a small intestine infected with cryptosporidium (green dots), a pathogenic parasite that is usually transmitted by contaminated water or milk.

its host than viruses because it cannot live independently. Along with needing a host in order to reproduce, a parasite completely depends on its host for survival. The host provides it with shelter, nourishment, and growth. One example of a pathogenic parasite is cryptosporidium (often called crypto), a parasite that causes a waterborne illness known as cryptosporidiosis. Like many other pathogens, crypto is found in water that has been contaminated by human or animal fecal matter. This includes lakes, rivers, ponds, and other bodies of freshwater, as well as swimming pools and drinking water that have not been properly filtered and treated.

People become infected with crypto when they swallow water that has been contaminated by cryptosporidium. Once the parasites are in someone's body, they travel to the small intestine and release tiny spores that burrow into the intestinal walls and then begin to multiply. Someone with a healthy immune system can often fight off the parasite, which means that symptoms fade away in a relatively short time or never develop

A Killer Amoeba

It is extremely rare for a microscopic water-dwelling amoeba known as *Naegleria fowleri* to infect humans—but when it does, the person almost always dies. *Naegleria fowleri* thrives in bodies of freshwater such as rivers, lakes, and ponds. In the United States it is most prevalent in the South, where summers are long and hot and water gets very warm from the sun. People typically become infected when they jump or dive into water and the amoeba is forced into the nose. It travels up through the sinuses and into the brain and spinal cord, where it causes *primary amoebic meningoencephalitis*, a devastating illness that rapidly destroys brain tissue. Says Jonathan Yoder, the CDC's waterborne disease coordinator: "It causes a great deal of trauma and a great deal of damage. It's a tragic infection."

According to the CDC, *Naegleria fowleri* infection was responsible for thirty-two deaths in the United States between 2001 and 2010, and three more were reported in 2011. During that summer, the deadly amoeba claimed the lives of two little boys aged seven and nine and a sixteen-year-old girl.

Quoted in Madison Park. "Brain-Eating Amoebas Blamed in Three Deaths." CNN, August 17, 2011. www.cnn.com/2011/HEALTH/08/17/amoeba.kids.deaths.

at all. For those with weakened immune systems, however, the parasite remains in the body, continues to multiply, and can lead to a severe case of cryptosporidiosis. Symptoms of the illness, such as abdominal cramps, nausea, vomiting, fever, and diarrhea, typically develop within two to ten days after the infestation occurs.

Although most infestations occur in bodies of freshwater, cryptosporidium has also been found in swimming pools. The parasite is chlorine-resistant, meaning that it can survive in pools even when chlorination is at normal levels. One such infestation was discovered in late March 2012, when a crypto outbreak in Duluth, Minnesota, was traced to a popular water park. An investigation found that more than forty children and adults who had visited the park developed cryptosporidiosis. Once the outbreak was discovered, the owners of the water park closed the facility to the public and treated the water with super-high levels of chlorine to kill the parasites.

A City's Nightmare

The outbreak at the Duluth water park was not a crisis situation, because the infestation was confined to one location and was brought under control quickly. But when cryptosporidium gets into a public drinking water supply, it can escalate into a community health emergency. This is what happened in 1993, when Milwaukee, Wisconsin, was the site of the largest and most severe documented outbreak of waterborne illness in U.S. history. In early April 1993 the health department began receiving dozens of telephone calls about a mysterious illness with symptoms that included fever, vomiting, abdominal cramps, and severe diarrhea. Local businesses reported unusually high employee absenteeism due to the illness, as did schools and hospitals throughout the city. On the basis of the symptoms described, health officials suspected that the culprit was contaminated drinking water, most likely due to a parasitic infestation.

Testing confirmed the presence of cryptosporidium at Milwaukee's southern water treatment plant, which was immediately shut down. The health department issued public advisories in which they urged citizens to boil water before use in order to kill the parasites. These precautions came too late, however, as the illness was already spreading throughout the city. Milwaukee physician Ian Gilson explains: "Ultimately by the time it was called a waterborne epidemic we knew we had a big problem on our hands."[4]

More than four hundred thousand people were sickened during the Milwaukee outbreak, and hundreds required hospitalization. One hundred three people died, of whom nearly all were suffering from acquired immune deficiency syndrome

(AIDS). The disease had severely weakened their immune systems and left them unable to fight off the infection. To this day Milwaukee health officials are not exactly sure how cryptosporidium got into the water. The most likely scenario, according to a report published in 1995, is that the parasites originated in Lake Michigan (from which Milwaukee obtains its water) and were able to pass through filters at the water plant.

A Chronic Parasitic Disease

For such a serious outbreak of waterborne illness to occur in the United States is highly unusual. The same is not true, however, of developing countries, where much-worse outbreaks are commonplace. One example is the parasitic illness schistosomiasis, which sickens an estimated 300 million people every year. Schistosomiasis is known as a neglected tropical disease, meaning it is confined to tropical regions of the world, such as South America, Africa, Asia, and the Middle East. It is also known as snail fever because it is caused by the parasitic worm schistosoma, which lives in tiny freshwater-dwelling snails. The worm lays eggs inside the snail, and when the eggs hatch, the larvae (known as cercariae) emerge and swim through the water to seek out a human or other mammal to serve as a host. A 2010 article by the International Association for Medical Assistance to Travelers describes this process:

> Like divers jumping from their boats, the cercariae, stimulated by the bright light and the high temperature of the day, abandon the snails to attack humans. Seen under the microscope they look like miniature tadpoles, with a pear shaped [body] and a long tail terminating in a y-shaped fork which acts as a propeller to move the organism through the water. They are now swimming in a desperate race against time, searching for a human host to ensure their survival. They will die within 48 hours if the search fails.[5]

When people wade, swim, or bathe in water that is infested with cercariae, the organisms are attracted to the oily secretions from human skin. They swim toward a prospective host and attach themselves with suckers, and then emit a chemical that forms a tiny hole in the skin. The cercariae burrow through the hole, and once inside the host they grow and develop into adult worms that live in the blood vessels. The worms mate in the bloodstream, and females deposit hundreds of eggs in the walls of the intestines and bladder. About half of the eggs are passed out of the body in feces or urine, while the rest become stuck in body tissue. They are recognized as foreign material and attacked by the immune system, and this reaction to the eggs is what causes schistosomiasis symptoms such as fever, chills, abdominal pain, fatigue, and muscle aches.

In the most severe cases, worms enter the central nervous system and lay their eggs in the brain or spinal cord. This result in inflammation (irritation and swelling) of the spinal cord, seizures, paralysis, and in some instances death. According to the WHO, schistosomiasis claims the lives of about 280,000 people each year, most of them living in African countries.

The cycle of schistosomiasis, or snail fever, is shown here. Snails pass organisms into water that burrow into human skin, invading the bloodstream and organs and developing into flukes. Fluke eggs are excreted by humans where they again infect snails.

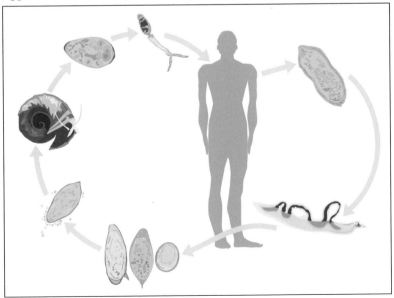

A Leading Killer

Though schistosomiasis kills hundreds of thousands each year, it is not the most deadly waterborne disease. The combined death toll of diarrheal disease is markedly higher than that of schistosomiasis. According to the humanitarian relief organization UNICEF (United Nations Children's Fund), each year more than 4 billion cases of diarrheal disease worldwide cause 2.2 million deaths, and an estimated three-fourths of those who die are children under age five. Diarrheal disease is an umbrella term that refers to a group of illnesses of which diarrhea (frequent, liquid bowel movements) is the primary symptom. When someone suffers from diarrhea, it usually indicates an infection in the intestinal tract caused by bacteria, viruses, or parasites. People can develop different types of diarrhea, depending on which pathogen has infected them. One type, bloody diarrhea (often called dysentery) is a symptom of enteritis, which is an inflammation of the small intestine. Three types of bacteria that are associated with this illness are shigella, E. coli, and salmonella. Another type of diarrhea, acute (meaning "abrupt") watery diarrhea, may be caused by a viral pathogen known as rotavirus, as well as by several types of bacteria, including *Vibrio cholerae*.

Of all the diarrheal diseases, none is more deadly than cholera. People develop it after ingesting contaminated water, but most are unaware of the infection because they never get sick. This is largely because *Vibrio cholerae* are sensitive to acid and often die when coming into contact with digestive acids in the stomach. But in people who ingest a large amount of contaminated water, or those whose immune systems are too weak to fight off the infection, the bacteria move into the small intestine. They begin to multiply rapidly, stimulating the production of a deadly toxin known as CTX.

The toxin binds to the intestinal walls, where it interferes with the normal flow of electrolytes, which are essential mineral ions such as sodium, potassium, and chloride. As a result, the body expels enormous amounts of water in the form of diarrhea, and this can lead to a dangerous state of dehydration.

The warning signs that someone is dehydrated include intense thirst, glassy or sunken eyes, little or no urine output, irregular heartbeat, and skin that is dry, shriveled, and slow to return to normal when pinched. If the person is not rehydrated with fluids immediately, death can occur within hours. Says Vanessa Rouzier, a physician who works with a medical group in Haiti: "It's shocking to see somebody die of dehydration. I saw a young 20-year-old collapse in front of me from paralysis because he had lost too much potassium. A healthy, strapping 20-year-old!"[6] Among people who die from cholera, the actual cause of death is nearly always dehydration.

A Ferocious Fever

Typhoid fever is another of the diarrheal diseases and also carries the risk of potentially deadly dehydration. Worldwide, typhoid affects more than 16 million people each year and kills an estimated 600,000. People contract the illness by drinking water or eating food that has been contaminated by a bacterium called *Salmonella typhi*, found in human feces. When someone is infected, the bacteria invade the small intestine and enter the bloodstream. They travel to the liver, gall bladder, spleen, and bone marrow, where they multiply in the cells of the organs and then reenter the bloodstream. In addition to diarrhea, typhoid symptoms include high fever, chest congestion, headache, abdominal pain, severe fatigue, and an overall achiness. Some people with typhoid develop a rash known as rose spots, which are small red spots that cover the abdomen and chest.

Typhoid is extremely rare in the United States; according to the National Institutes of Health, fewer than four hundred cases are reported each year. These are almost exclusively among people who have traveled to developing areas of the world where the illness is common, such as Mexico and South American countries. This was the case with a woman named Indigo, who contracted typhoid in 2005 while vacationing in Mexico. The illness made her sicker than she had ever been in her life, as she writes:

The day of my return, I became violently ill. I had uncontrollable diarrhea and vomiting. My fever shot up to 104 degrees, and I was hospitalized where I remained for seven days. I was packed on ice continually as my fever shot to 105. I suffered convulsions. The pain in my body was so excruciating. I was put on a morphine drip, and I have a high tolerance for pain. Blood tests showed minimal kidney function and liver failure. Even after I was released, I continued to have fevers of 104 and 105. I was disabled by this illness for months.[7]

The Discovery of "Little Animals"

Today a great deal is known about bacteria, viruses, and protozoa, but centuries ago scientists had no idea the organisms existed. That changed in the 1600s when a Dutch fabric merchant named Antoni van Leeuwenhoek discovered bacteria. He often used a magnifying glass to inspect the quality of his cloth, and one day he decided to use it to examine drops of rainwater. To his amazement and delight, he observed that the water was not still—it was alive, teeming with tiny organisms that he referred to as "little animals." In an October 1676 letter to the Royal Society of London, Van Leeuwenhoek wrote: "[It] was for me, among all the marvels that I have discovered in nature, the most marvellous of all; and I must say, for my part, that no more pleasant sight has ever yet come before my eyes than this of so many thousands of living creatures in one small drop of water, all huddling and moving, but each creature having its own motion."

Van Leeuwenhoek was dismayed when his finding was met with ridicule and mockery rather than enthusiasm. Yet he had no doubt about what he had seen, and he refused to let skepti-

Vicious Viruses

The woman's frightening bout with liver failure is characteristic of the most severe form of typhoid fever. It is also a risk associated with the illness known as hepatitis, whose name means "inflammation of the liver." Scientists have identified five types of hepatitis: A, B, C, D, and E. The two waterborne types are hepatitis A and E, both of which are caused by viruses that originate in human fecal matter. Hepatitis A, which is the less severe of the two, is relatively common in the United

cism discourage him. Throughout the remainder of his life, he continued to study the "little animals" and meticulously documented his discoveries. He is now credited with making a major contribution toward a scientific understanding of bacteria and other microorganisms.

Quoted in Douglas Anderson. "Counting the Animalcules." Lens on Leeuwenhoek, September 1, 2009. http://lensonleeuwenhoek.net/counting.htm.

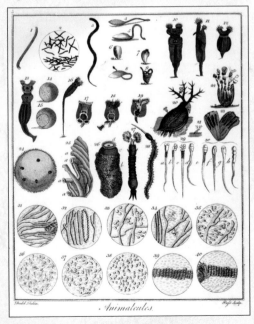

Antoni van Leeuwenhoek made drawings of bacteria, which he called "little animals," that he saw in drops of water through his magnifying glass.

States, whereas hepatitis E is found mostly in African, Asian, and South American countries.

When someone has been infected with a hepatitis virus, symptoms usually develop within two to six weeks. These include an abrupt onset of fever, body weakness, nausea, abdominal discomfort, and jaundice, which is a yellowing of the skin and whites of the eyes caused by poor liver function. Hepatitis can range in severity from a mild case that runs its course in a few weeks to a more serious infection that lasts for months. Nearly all people who develop hepatitis A or E recover completely with no long-term effects, but in some cases the illness is much more dangerous. It can occasionally progress into what is known as fulminant acute hepatitis, a life-threatening condition in which the liver becomes so severely inflamed that it fails. The majority of people who develop this condition do not survive—up to 90 percent of those with fulminant acute hepatitis die within weeks or even days.

A Global Problem

Every year, in countries throughout the world, millions of people are sickened by waterborne illnesses. These illnesses may be caused by bacteria, viruses, or parasites, and they range in severity from relatively mild symptoms that fade after a short time to dehydration, severe organ damage, and death. Although each illness has its own unique characteristics, in one way they are all the same: None of them would exist without contaminated water.

CHAPTER TWO

The Consequences of Human Actions

O ver the years, lakes, rivers, ponds, and streams throughout the world have become badly polluted by human and animal waste matter. This has happened for numerous reasons, including inadequate sanitation systems, poor hygiene practices (such as open defecation), and careless farming methods. People may not always know about the role they play in making water unfit for human use. This is especially true in the world's poorest countries, where there is low awareness of the connection between water contamination and health. But human actions are largely responsible for the widespread sickness and death that result from waterborne illness.

Deplorable Sanitation

In the developing world, one of the biggest contributors to water contamination is inadequate sanitation. Many regions of developing countries, including both rural and urban, either lack any type of sanitation at all or have aging, crumbling systems with sewage pipes that are cracked and broken. Fecal material leaks out of the pipes and is washed into streams and rivers during heavy rains. The waste also seeps through the soil to pollute groundwater, which is a source of water that is stored deep beneath the surface in the spaces between rocks. As a result of this contamination, disease-causing pathogens are present in the water that people use for drinking, bathing, and cooking, which inevitably leads to outbreaks of waterborne illness. In regions that suffer from severe water shortages, the risk is especially high. People become so desperate for water that they are willing to drink from any source they can find. This is true even if they know that the water is not clean and could possibly harm them.

In many places in the world people become so desperate for water that they are willing to drink from any source they can find.

Michael Onyango understands this kind of desperation. He lives with his wife and two-year-old daughter in a poverty-stricken area of Nairobi, the capital city of Kenya. After going for days without water, and having no money to buy some from a vendor, Onyango was delighted when he noticed water gushing from a burst pipe. He called to his wife to help him gather as much as possible in buckets. The water did not appear to be clean, but Onyango was too desperate to care about that. "All my family needed was water," he says. "To us, the source did not matter."[8] Within a few days of drinking the water and using it for bathing, Onyango, his wife, and little girl began vomiting, developed severe diarrhea, and broke out in rashes that covered their bodies. They went to a neighborhood clinic, where all three were diagnosed with typhoid fever and amoebic dysentery, an intestinal disease caused by a water-dwelling amoeba (a type of protozoan, or single-celled organism) known as *Entamoeba histolytica*. Onyango was shocked when he learned that the pipe he thought was gushing water had actually been carrying sewage.

Illnesses caused by exposure to contaminated water are common in any country that suffers from a combination of severe water shortages and inadequate sanitation. One example is the Caribbean island nation of Haiti. At least half the population has no access to clean water, and sanitation there is considered to be among the worst in the Western Hemisphere. The capital city of Port-au-Prince, which is home to 3 million people, has no sewage system at all. The families who have latrines on their property hire workers to clean them—and in the process of cleaning, the city's water often becomes even more contaminated than it already is. Working at night these "bayakous" descend into deep holes in the ground and use their hands to scoop excrement into buckets. Then they haul the waste matter to the nearest canals and dump it into the water.

Yet only the wealthiest citizens in Port-au-Prince are fortunate enough to have latrines of their own. The majority of people who live there cannot afford such luxuries, so they simply use the ground as their toilet. In a practice known as open defecation, they have bowel movements (defecate) along the banks of streams or rivers, on railroad tracks, or behind bushes and trees. During periods of heavy rain, such as monsoon season, this human waste is washed into the river and canals, where it contaminates water that people depend on for drinking. Says physician Louise Ivers, who is chief of mission for the humanitarian organization Partners in Health: "There is no effective public water system in Haiti. The river is the place where bathing, drinking and defecation all occur."[9]

Unimaginable Filth

Haiti is one of numerous regions of the world where open defecation is a common, accepted practice. According to a 2012 report by UNICEF, 15 percent of the global population—more than 1 billion people—regularly defecate outside. In her book *The Big Necessity: The Unmentionable World of Human Waste and Why It Matters*, Rose George candidly discusses the absence of sanitation in these regions and the magnitude of the open defecation problem. She writes:

> Four in ten people have no access to any latrine, toilet, bucket, or box. Nothing. Instead they defecate by train tracks and in forests. They do it in plastic bags and fling them through the air in narrow slum alleyways. . . . Four in ten people live in situations where they are surrounded by human excrement because it is in the bushes outside their village or in their city yards, left by children outside the backdoor. It is tramped back in on their feet, carried on fingers onto clothes, food, and drinking water.[10]

The 2012 UNICEF report states that open defecation is most prevalent in southern Asia, where 55 percent of the population regularly defecates outdoors. One Asian country where this is a common practice is Pakistan, as the humanitarian organization Plan Pakistan explains:

> People young and old, healthy and infirm, male and female are forced to use the great outdoors as their [toilet], making use of bushes, riverbanks, open fields and small

groves. Not only are open-defecation sites smelly and unsightly, but the resultant contamination of water supplies causes disease as villagers blithely use untreated water, assuming that clean to the eye means clean in an absolute sense.[11]

A 2012 article on the website Pure Pakistan tells of a woman named Shazma who lives with her nine children in the Pakistani village of Balandi. The family has always defecated outside and had no idea that this was contaminating the water supply. Nor did they know that their skin infections, diarrhea, and other intestinal illnesses were caused by drinking water that contained their own excrement.

Bangladesh is another South Asian country where open defecation is a common practice, and waterborne illnesses are widespread there as well. A humanitarian worker named Jane Bean works with people in a remote Bangladeshi village and has observed firsthand the effects of poor sanitation on the

A street in Haiti with an incomplete drainage canal filled with rubbish and sewage. In Haiti, four in ten people practice open defecation because they have no access to toilets or latrines.

environment and people's health. She describes "the powerful stench of human excreta" that blows through the windows of the hut where she stays, and she has seen people openly defecate along the banks of the river and in other parts of the village. Referring to the global incidence of this problem, Bean writes: "The result is that millions of people all over the world are drinking their own waste. . . . This horror is killing millions."[12]

The "Flying Toilets" of Kibera

Open defecation typically refers to the practice of defecating on the ground, but the term is also used to describe what are known as "flying toilets." This term refers to the practice of defecating inside one's home in a plastic bag and then dispos-

Making Wastewater

Throughout the world one of the main sources of water contamination is wastewater. This is a combination of sewage (human excrement and urine), gray water (from kitchen use and bathing), wastewater from hospitals and other institutions, industrial liquid waste (known as effluent), agricultural runoff, and wastewater from horticulture. According to a 2010 report by the United Nations Environment Programme, more than 90 percent of all wastewater in developing countries is discharged untreated into rivers, lakes, and/or oceans. This has a significant impact on human health and is a primary contributor to waterborne illness.

Just one liter of wastewater can contain thousands or even millions of disease-causing pathogens such as *Cryptosporidium parvum, Salmonella, Entamoeba histolytica, Vibrio cholerae,* and viruses, as well as numerous others. Because of the dangers posed by these pathogens to human populations, there is a pressing need for wastewater pollution to stop. The authors of the 2010 report write: "The global population is expected to exceed nine billion people by 2050. Major growth will take place in developing of the bag by tossing it onto a trash heap or simply flinging it out the door and onto the ground. This is common in many areas of the developing world, such as the Nairobi slum of Kibera. Only property owners have toilets, and anyone who wants to use them must pay for the privilege. This is simply not affordable for most Kibera residents because they are so poor. Some community toilets are available, but people often have to walk long distances to reach them. Also, many of these toilets are so overfilled with excrement that they have been abandoned and are no longer usable. So most Kibera residents find flying toilets to be the best option for relieving themselves. As one female resident explains: "I think that over half of the population uses this method."[13]

ing countries, particularly in urban areas that already have inadequate wastewater infrastructure. The financial, environmental and social costs are projected to increase dramatically unless wastewater management receives urgent attention."

E. Corcoran, C. Nellemann, E. Baker, R. Bos, D. Osborn, and H. Savelli. *Sick Water? The Central Role of Wastewater Management in Sustainable Development.* United Nations Environment Programme and UN-Habitat, 2010. www.unep.org/pdf/Sick Water_screen.pdf.

Just one liter of wastewater can contain millions of disease-causing pathogens.

The woman is a health-care worker, so she is very aware of the health risks of disposing waste in such an unhygienic way. But even she does it because she feels like it is her only option. "I find myself going back to using flying toilets because that is the only alternative I have," she says. "At night, it is so dark in Kibera that you cannot dare to get out of your room since you are not sure if you will fall in one of the abandoned toilets and, as a woman, you can never be sure that you will not be raped. . . . Therefore, for women, the best option is to use flying toilets at night." Still, the woman becomes frustrated with the human filth throughout the village. "You wake up in the morning, you cannot get out of your door," she says, "and by 5 am you find heaps and heaps of flying toilets at your front door. We just have to clean them to get out of the houses."[14] Even more disturbing is that children pick the bags of excrement off the ground and toss them to each other as though they were playing with balls.

Flying toilets contaminate Kibera's water supply in a number of ways. People toss the bags onto rooftops, where they break open and splatter the excrement around. During the rainy season, when residents harvest rooftop rainwater for drinking, they are gathering water that has been contaminated by feces and is unsafe for use. Also during the rainy season, all the excrement-filled bags that litter the ground are washed into the surrounding rivers, which serve as a primary source of water for Kibera residents.

Animal-Waste Contamination

Unhygienic practices like open defecation and tossing bags of excrement on the ground may seem inconceivable to people in the industrialized world. They consider toilets to be one of life's necessities, rather than a luxury. They also take for granted that clean, safe drinking water will be available just by turning on a faucet. Yet even though industrialized countries have modern facilities for treating drinking water, as well as sanitation systems for handling human waste, disease-causing pathogens can still end up in water supplies. Because of this, developed countries often struggle with waterborne illnesses, too.

Livestock waste is known to contain pathogens such as salmonella, E. coli, cryptosporidium, and the viruses that cause influenza and hepatitis.

Agriculture, for instance, is a significant contributor to waterborne illness in the United States. In fact, the EPA says that agricultural runoff is the single largest source of water pollution in America's rivers and streams. Runoff occurs when rain or melted snow cannot be absorbed and held by the soil, so it runs over the ground and washes into streams, rivers, and lakes. This includes pollution from pesticides used on croplands and manure from livestock, which is commonly applied to soil as an organic fertilizer. Livestock waste is known to contain pathogens such as salmonella, E. coli, cryptosporidium, and viruses that cause hepatitis and influenza. If too much waste is spread over the land, these pathogens can wash into surface water and groundwater during rainstorms. According to the EPA, nearly 20 million Americans become sick each year from these and other pathogens that originate in animal waste.

The biggest risk of agriculture-related water contamination comes from concentrated animal feeding operations, which are often called CAFOs or factory farms. These massive operations house thousands, and even tens of thousands, of animals that collectively produce 500 million tons (454 million t) of manure each year—three times the amount of human waste that is generated annually in the United States. Says the Natural Resources Defense Council: "Giant livestock farms, which can house hundreds of thousands of pigs, chickens, or cows, produce vast amounts of waste—often generating the waste equivalent of a small city. While a problem of this nature—and scale—sounds almost comical, pollution from livestock farms seriously threatens humans, fish and ecosystems."[15] The council and other environmental groups say that the bigger the farming operation, the greater the risk for water contamination.

Tragedy in New York

Though large farming operations are more likely to pollute water supplies, smaller farms have also been shown to contaminate water. A single gram of animal waste can contain millions of pathogens such as viruses, parasites, and bacteria, so even moderate-sized manure collection areas contribute to waterborne illness outbreaks. This proved to be true in late August 1999, when E. coli contaminated a portion of the water supply at the Washington County Fair in upstate New York. Most water that was used during the fair was supplied by a large tank of chlorinated water that was fed by a network of deep wells. But because the area had gone through a serious drought, fair officials were finding it a challenge to keep the tank filled. So they decided to supplement the water supply by drawing from a shallow well. They furnished that water to vendors on the west side of the fair for use in making beverages and ice. At the time, no one had any idea that the well water contained a vicious, deadly pathogen known as E. coli O157:H7.

In early September, shortly after the fair had ended, the New York State Department of Public Health began to receive reports about children who were hospitalized after developing bloody diarrhea. The reports continued to escalate as more children, as well as adults, became ill. A September 1999 *New York Times* article explains: "One after another, then by the dozens, they went to local hospitals and doctors' offices,

Pathogens Go Swimming, Too

During the summer months, when people spend the most time swimming, the risk for waterborne illnesses increases. After an outbreak has occurred, there is often confusion over how the pathogens were able to enter the water. The usual suspects are sewage overflow and agricultural runoff, but recreational water (including swimming pools) can become contaminated by sources that are much less obvious—such as the swimmers themselves. The CDC explains:

> Swimmers share the water—and the germs in it—with every person who enters the pool. On average, people have about 0.14 grams of feces on their bottoms which, when rinsed off, can contaminate recreational water. In addition, when someone is ill with diarrhea, their stool can contain millions of germs. This means that just one person with diarrhea can easily contaminate the water in a large pool or water park.

Centers for Disease Control and Prevention. "Where Are Recreational Water Illnesses (RWIs) Found?," November 9, 2011. www.cdc.gov/healthywater/swimming/rwi/rwi-where.html.

Just one person with diarrhea can easily contaminate the water in a large pool or water park.

howling with stomach cramps, weakened by diarrhea and nausea, some near death. Parents and grandparents got sick, too, baffled that something that had seemed so wholesome could turn out this badly."[16] An investigation by state health officials found that all those who were sick had obtained beverages from the same vendors, and the contamination was traced to the shallow well. A follow-up report stated that after a heavy rainstorm in late August, the well had likely been polluted by runoff from the youth cattle shed where about one hundred cows were kept. As many as five thousand children and adults were sickened by the E. coli, and two of the victims died. One was seventy-nine-year-old Wayne Wester, and the other was a three-year-old girl named Rachel Aldrich.

Prolific Pollution

From broken sewer lines and unhygienic human practices to pathogenic bacteria in animal waste, water can become contaminated in numerous ways. In many cases people are not aware that the water they drink, cook with, and use for bathing contains disease-causing pathogens that can make them sick and possibly even kill them. Nor do they necessarily know that their own practices are largely responsible for water contamination. Although developing countries struggle the most with waterborne illness, it is a problem all over the world—one that will not go away until the human actions that cause it are stopped.

CHAPTER THREE

Where Human Suffering Is Greatest

Although waterborne illnesses have been identified in every part of the world, the highest prevalence—and the greatest amount of suffering—is in developing countries. In his book *The Blue Death*, Robert D. Morris discusses the widespread devastation that results from these illnesses and uses an analogy to illustrate how dire the situation is for people in the developing world. "Like a tsunami in slow motion," Morris writes, "unsafe drinking water is killing constantly; almost forty thousand people will die this week alone. Unlike a tsunami, it never stops."[17] There are numerous reasons why suffering is so great in developing countries, the most obvious of which is widespread poverty. People are severely malnourished, and their bodies are weak and unable to fight off sickness. Other factors include severe shortages of clean water, poor sanitation, and unhygienic living conditions. The contaminated water people drink causes a wide range of waterborne illnesses, with the most common—and the most dangerous—being diarrheal disease.

Waterborne Enemies

The primary reason diarrheal diseases are so dangerous is that they carry an enormous risk of death from dehydration. The rate of diarrhea is greatest in regions where the poverty rate is exceptionally high and people have no choice but to use water that is contaminated by disease-causing pathogens. Most threatened by dehydration are children under age five. This is because their bodies are smaller, water makes up a greater proportion of their body weight, and their kidneys are less able to conserve water compared with older children and adults. According to a 2009 report by UNICEF, nearly one in five childhood deaths is due to some form of diarrheal disease. The report's authors write: "It kills more young children than AIDS, malaria and measles *combined.*"[18]

More than 80 percent of childhood diarrheal deaths occur in African and South Asian countries, with a significant majority of those deaths in India. Of fifteen countries with the highest annual number of childhood diarrheal deaths, India has been ranked number one by UNICEF. Every year more than 386,000 Indian children die from diarrheal illnesses, compared with 151,700 in Nigeria, 82,100 in Afghanistan, and 53,300 in Pakistan. One of the most prevalent diarrheal illnesses in India is cholera. It kills thousands of people each year, including adults as well as children, and is most common in the poorest areas of the country, where the water people use is contaminated by human waste.

This is a massive problem in Orissa, a poverty-stricken state that is located on India's eastern coast. Says Paranga Majhi, who lives in a small village in Orissa: "We don't have any source of safe drinking water. So we are forced to use water from dirty rivers and ponds. That's why we are falling ill."[19] Continuous use of this unclean water has led to numerous cholera outbreaks throughout Orissa, such as one that began in August 2010 in the Rayagada district. The deadly disease affected more than one thousand people across three hundred villages in Orissa, killing at least 140 of the victims.

An Ongoing Nightmare

As in India, suffering from waterborne illness is widespread in the African country of Zimbabwe. UNICEF reports that more than 4 million people in Zimbabwe live in high-risk areas, meaning those where water is not safe to drink and sanitary

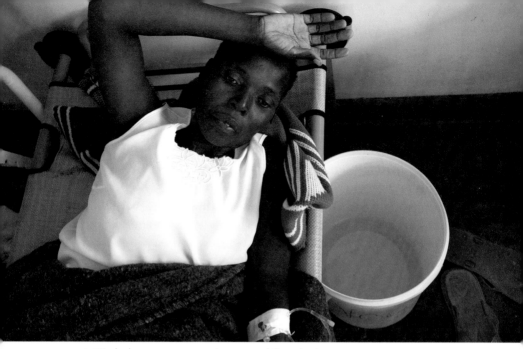

A Zimbabwean woman is treated for cholera at a treatment center. The 2008 cholera epidemic in Zimbabwe killed forty thousand people and infected nearly one hundred thousand others.

practices are extremely poor. The combination of contaminated water and poor hygiene has led to numerous outbreaks of waterborne illnesses in the country, such as in August 2008. That marked the beginning of a devastating outbreak of cholera in Zimbabwe that lasted for more than a year. The epidemic, which was declared a national emergency, killed at least forty thousand people and infected nearly one hundred thousand others. A major reason why the cholera epidemic killed so many people in Zimbabwe is that most of those who caught the illness were already weakened by hunger and disease, including HIV/AIDS. In addition, political instability and an economic crisis in the nation led to severe shortages of chemicals used for water treatment, inadequate supplies of medicines, and a shortage of qualified health-care providers.

The Zimbabwean province of Mashonaland West was among the hardest-hit areas during the cholera epidemic. There, as elsewhere in the country, the youngest victims were the most vulnerable to becoming ill. In December 2008, in the middle of the night, a nine-year-old girl named Sarah began showing symptoms that were characteristic of cholera. Because the local clinic had run out of funding, it was closed down, and the only other clinic was three hours away. So, desperate to get help for his little girl, Sarah's father walked the entire distance carrying her on his back. She was already undernourished when she contracted cholera and, according to the clinic doctor, she was also infected with malaria. With her body weakened by the effects of malnutrition and disease, Sarah's condition was extremely critical, and she died that evening. Her parents could not help thinking she might still be alive if the clinic in their village had not closed down. They were devastated by the loss of their child—and by the fact that her body was handed back to them wrapped in heavy plastic to prevent the spread of disease. "If I had at least been able to see her one more time," says Sarah's mother, "it would have helped me grieve. I don't know how to tell the other children what has happened."[20]

Zimbabwe's cholera epidemic was officially declared to be over in 2009, but sporadic outbreaks of other waterborne illnesses have continued in both urban and rural areas of the country. In January 2012, for example, about nine hundred people in the capital city of Harare and its outlying areas contracted typhoid. Yet despite the consistent prevalence of waterborne illness, an estimated one-third of Zimbabweans still obtain their drinking water from unprotected sources. It is a common perception among these residents that since the yearlong cholera epidemic is over, they no longer have anything to worry about.

Barbra Phiri, a single mother who lives in a rural area about 28 miles (45km) southwest of Harare, is among the many Zimbabweans who believe that waterborne illness is something from the past. Phiri allows her two-year-old twins to play in a pool of green water near her hut; just a few yards away sits an overflowing latrine. Although Phiri's first child died from diarrhea in 2010, she does not fully understand what caused the baby to get sick. Nor does she recognize the connection between the water her twins play in and their health, even though they suffer from skin infections and frequent recurrences of diarrhea. "We don't use dirty water for drinking or cooking," she says. "We get clean water from the dam or the wells, so how can our children die from waterborne diseases?"[21]

Plight of a War-Torn Country

Since 2003 Iraq has been embroiled in war, and this has caused turmoil and suffering for the people who live there. The conflict has destroyed the country's infrastructure, including most water purification plants, which has led to a severe shortage of clean water. Thus, the Iraqi people have become dependent on the Tigris and Euphrates Rivers, whose water is polluted. According to the humanitarian agency CARE International, about 2.2 million tons (2 million t) of raw sewage is dumped into the rivers each day—four times the amount that entered the rivers before the war. Throughout Iraq, use of this contaminated water has vastly increased the incidence of waterborne illness.

Representatives from UNICEF visited Iraq in 2008 and interviewed more than nine thousand families. The group found that only 31 percent of households had access to safe drinking water, and less than 35 percent of households had a sanitary way to dispose of human waste. With this lack of safe water and sanitation, Iraq has seen a sharp rise in cholera, dysentery, hepatitis, polio, and typhoid, especially among young children. In the most deprived Iraqi communities, more than half of children under age five have suffered from a diarrheal disease, and this remains a significant cause of child mortality.

Sewage and trash line the streets of a poor neighborhood in war-torn Baghdad, Iraq.

Plagued by a Parasite

This lack of understanding about the risks of waterborne illness is typical among people in remote areas of the developing world, and it contributes to a higher prevalence of disease. Many are unaware, for instance, of the dangers posed by the parasitic disease schistosomiasis as well as how common it is in developing countries. In the West African country of Ghana, an abundance of the tiny snails that carry the schistosoma parasite thrive in an enormous freshwater lake called Lake Volta. Young people who swim, wade, or bathe in the lake are especially vulnerable and the most likely to be infected. In some villages around Lake Volta, more than 90 percent of the

A male and female pair of schistosoma worms is shown here magnified. The female lives in a groove on the male's back. People who swim, wade, or bathe in infected waters are especially vulnerable to such parasites.

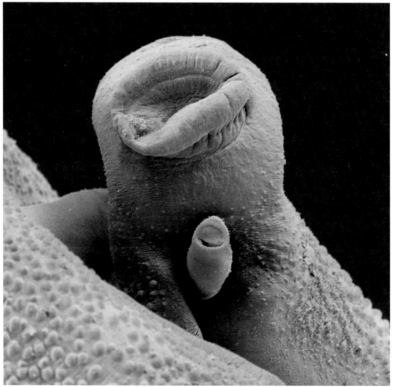

children have developed schistosomiasis. The disease can damage internal organs and impair children's growth and cognitive development. An October 2010 article in the online magazine *Pacific Standard* explains: "It stunts children's growth, affects their memory and IQ, and keeps them out of school."[22]

Medical treatment brings improvement in schistosomiasis symptoms, but people are often not aware of how the disease is transmitted, so they can easily become reinfected if they again swim or bathe in contaminated water. Also, many who contract the illness do not receive treatment at all. The WHO estimates that about 200 million people in Africa, Asia, and South America are currently infected with schistosomiasis, yet fewer than 15 percent receive treatment. One reason is that in many remote areas of developing countries, people have to travel great distances to reach the nearest hospital or clinic. In some areas people will turn instead to folk remedies to deal with ailments such as waterborne illnesses, often with devastating results. According to Medicine on the Move, an organization that provides medical care in West Africa, this lack of access to appropriate health care can lead to a needless loss of lives:

> In West Africa, many communities are remote and can be difficult to access. Villagers may have to travel long distances to reach professional clinics. In the absence of trained health professionals, many utilize traditional remedies—not all of which are reliable and some of which may result in further complications or infections. Consequently, many preventable morbidities and mortalities occur on a regular basis.[23]

Along with the problem of distance, another reason for the low treatment rate is that people with schistosomiasis may not realize they have it. Symptoms often do not appear for weeks or even months after infection. This lack of obvious, immediate warning signs can lead to severe health problems by the time the disease is detected. Even when symptoms are present (such as fever and blood in the urine), they are often not recognized by sufferers as a sign of a serious problem. Says

Jonathan Porter, cofounder of Medicine on the Move, "Many men see having blood their urine as a sign of virility, but doctors say it is a sign that the disease has eaten its way through the lower intestine."[24]

Suffering in the Philippines

Although schistosomiasis is most common in African countries, it also affects many other regions of the developing world, such as the Philippines. According to Emiliana Villacarillo, who is mayor of the small Philippine village of San Pascual, a June 2012 health examination of 543 residents in one area of the village found that all but one had contracted schistosomiasis. Those who were suffering from the illness ranged in age from two-year-old children to older adults. Says Villacarillo: "It is only the babies who are still carried by their parents and have not yet [walked] on the ground who are not affected by the disease."[25]

People in the Philippines also suffer from other waterborne illnesses such as typhoid fever. One large typhoid outbreak that began in March 2012 was particularly severe in the province of Cebu. Cases were reported throughout the province, including the southwestern town of Alegria and the centrally located Cebu City. By far the hardest-hit area was the northwestern town of Tuburan, which prompted health officials to declare a state of emergency. The number of typhoid cases in Tuburan reached nearly one thousand, and the local hospital became overcrowded. To help care for the staggering number of sick patients, the Philippine Army's 78th Infantry Battalion was called in to set up tents and folding beds in an area near the hospital.

According to the Philippine Department of Health, the reason the number of typhoid cases was so high in Tuburan is that only 41 percent of homes in the town have toilets or latrines. Many homes lack sanitation of any kind, so residents must dispose of their waste outside—which contaminates the water in reservoirs that people use for drinking, cooking, and bathing. To help remedy this problem, Tuburan health officials

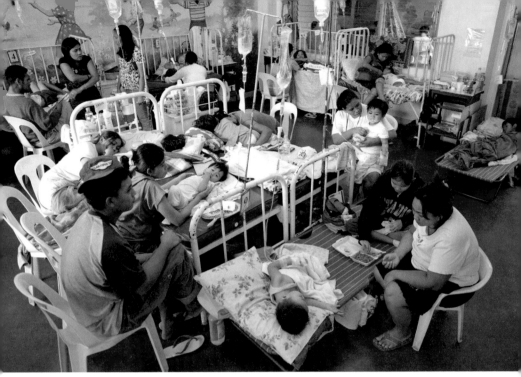

Filipino typhoid patients receive treatment at a medical center near Manila. In 2012, in some cities, the number of typhoid cases in the country skyrocketed to epidemic proportions.

installed filters and chlorinators at the three local reservoirs and planned to build two more reservoirs to help supply clean water. The officials also undertook efforts to educate residents about sanitation and proper hygiene to help prevent further outbreaks of typhoid and other waterborne illnesses.

"Our Country Is Not Safe"

Typhoid, cholera, and other waterborne illnesses are a serious, continuous health problem in the developing world. One illness that represents a growing threat is poliomyelitis (polio), which is a viral disease that is caused by the poliovirus. People become infected when they drink water that has been contaminated by the virus, and once it is inside their bodies, it quickly begins to multiply and spread. It is carried through the bloodstream and into the central nervous system, where it destroys neurons (nerve cells) that control the muscles needed for swallowing, breathing, circulation, and body movement. Sufferers are often left paralyzed, and many die.

Prior to the 1950s polio was rampant throughout the United States, and it paralyzed and/or killed tens of thousands of people, mostly children. The illness has long been extinct in most countries of the world because of vaccinations that prevent it—but it has not been wiped out completely. Polio still lingers in some developing nations, and in some areas the incidence is increasing. According to a 2012 study by the British National Institute of Biological Standards and Control, Pakistan reported 198 cases of polio in 2011 compared with 144 cases the prior year. In Afghanistan polio rose from 30 cases in 2010 to 81 cases in 2011. Researcher Philip Minor, who was involved in the study, says it is very possible that the illness could spread to areas that are now polio free. "Clearly," he says, "if one country has poliomyelitis the whole world is at risk."[26]

One example of polio spreading to a formerly polio-free nation occurred in Bangladesh. Because the country had been polio free for many years, the people of Bangladesh

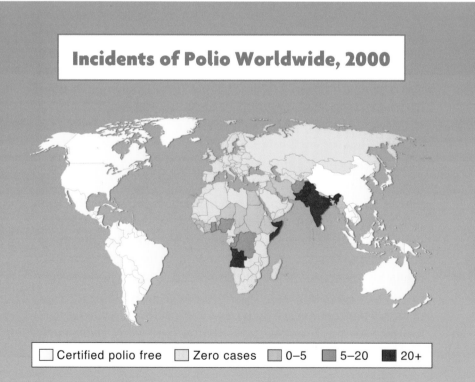

Incidents of Polio Worldwide, 2000

☐ Certified polio free ☐ Zero cases ☐ 0–5 ☐ 5–20 ■ 20+

Taken from: World Health Organization.

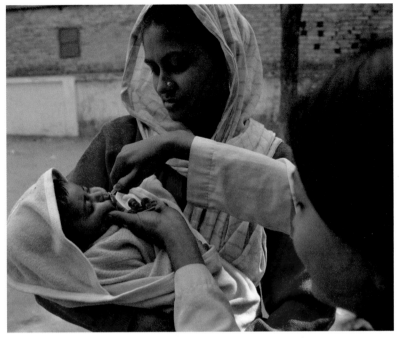

A Bangladeshi health care worker administers a polio vaccine at a vaccination center in Dhaka. Incidents of polio in Bangladesh have been blamed on polio cases in India and Pakistan.

believed the disease was completely eradicated. Tahmina Akhter, who lives in Chandpur, Bangladesh, was among those who had no fear that polio was a threat in her country. Then one morning in March 2006, Akhter's nine-year-old daughter, Rahima, fell ill. The little girl could not move her arms or legs, nor could she get out of bed. Over the next few days, Rahima suffered from extreme pain throughout her body. She was unable to raise her arms to feed herself and had to be spoon-fed by her mother. Because her legs were paralyzed, Rahima had to be carried from the bed to the toilet by her mother. At first Akhter thought Rahima's pain was the result of a table that had accidentally fallen on her. But as the days went by and the child continued to feel worse, it became obvious that something much more serious was going on. Still, Akhter was shocked when lab results came back positive for polio.

"I Have Never Felt So Much Pain"

People from industrialized countries often have no idea how horrendous cholera can be for those who suffer from it. Because it results from water contaminated by human waste, the illness is only prevalent in regions of the developing world that have poor sanitation. Yet if someone travels to one of these countries, the person may contract cholera and find out firsthand what a dreadful illness it is. This was the case with a writer from Utah named Steven Symes, who got sick while visiting the Central American country of Honduras. He writes:

> I never figured out how I became infected, although with the poor sanitary standards there were plenty of opportunities. I basically felt like I had a really, really bad flu. I could not keep anything in at either end and my appetite completely left me. It got to the point at about day five that I could not keep water or even Gatorade down. My body was weak, I was delirious and then I woke up on a table in a Honduran emergency room. . . . I cannot tell you how much the infection hurt. The day I went to the ER my whole body just coursed with pain, which echoed through my muscles, tendons and even my bones. I have never felt so much pain in my life; it was so much that I could not even hold still out of the sheer agony of it.

Steven Symes. "Cholera: My Personal Experience." *Steven Symes, Writer* (blog), May 23, 2012. http://writerstevensymes.blogspot.com/2012/05/cholera-my-personal-experience.html.

Rahima was the first confirmed case of polio in Bangladesh in more than five years. In the days before she became ill, her family had attended a wedding in India, and doctors traced the poliovirus that infected her to that country. Many experts believe that the presence of polio in neighboring countries represents a significant threat to the health of Bangladesh. Says health minister Matiur Rahman: "Our country is not safe, as neighbours India and Pakistan are not polio free."[27]

Tragic Reality

Although people in the industrialized world may not see waterborne illness as a serious threat, the fact remains that developing nations are plagued by these illnesses. Poverty, poor sanitation, water shortages, and even a simple lack of awareness can leave people in these countries vulnerable to contracting diseases that sicken and kill thousands every year. This disturbing trend is likely to continue as long as so many people still lack access to clean, safe water.

CHAPTER FOUR

Waterborne Illness Catastrophes

Wherever or whenever they occur, waterborne illness outbreaks are frightening because of the vast potential for sickness and death. But when paired with an unforeseen event such as a natural disaster, they can reach epidemic levels and throw a state or even an entire nation into mass turmoil. This is especially true when disasters hit the poorest developing countries. On a day-to-day basis, these countries already struggle with severe water shortages, poor sanitation, and health care that is inadequate to meet the needs of the people. So if an earthquake strikes or torrential rains lead to severe flooding, existing problems can grow exceedingly worse. Says WHO physician Guido Sabatinelli: "The lack of clean water and the unavailability of medication, in the aftermath of these floods, is a deadly combination. When added to the poor living conditions and the lack of food, which contribute to vulnerability, the picture is gruesome."[28] As clean water becomes scarcer, waterborne illness can spread rapidly, affecting so many people that it is impossible for health-care workers to help all or even most of them. These situations can quickly escalate into catastrophe.

A Deadly Rampage Begins

No country on earth illustrates this potential for a waterborne illness disaster better than Haiti. It is one of the world's most impoverished nations, with 80 percent of its people living in poverty. Over half the population has no access to clean water, sanitation is nonexistent or severely lacking countrywide, and it has the highest rate of infant and child deaths in the Western Hemisphere. So in January 2010, when Haiti was struck by the most powerful earthquake it had experienced in two hundred years, the devastation was beyond belief. Homes collapsed into rubble, thousands of schools were destroyed, roads buckled, and hospitals toppled over into ruin. More than two hundred thousand people were killed, and countless others were injured. Because of widespread food and water shortages, combined with the general chaos that reigned after the disaster, humanitarian organizations feared that it was only a matter of time before a serious disease epidemic broke out. What they could not have anticipated was an outbreak of cholera.

Although Haiti has had a long, ongoing struggle with waterborne illnesses, cholera was never before documented in the

Haitian cholera patients are treated at a Doctors Without Borders clinic in Haiti. For the first time in Haiti's history, the country was plagued by a cholera epidemic that began in October 2010.

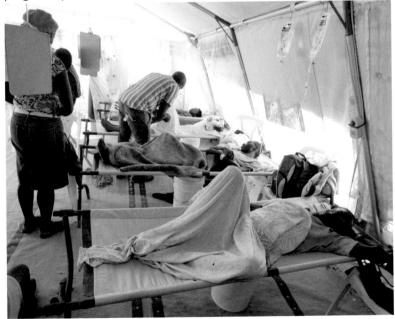

country. Even when a nineteenth-century cholera epidemic ravaged other Caribbean countries, including Jamaica, Puerto Rico, Trinidad, Cuba, the Bahamas, and the Dominican Republic, Haiti was somehow spared. Because of that history, health officials had no reason to fear a cholera outbreak after the 2010 earthquake, and they assured the Haitian people that cholera was not a risk. Such assurance came from the United States as well. In March 2010 the CDC posted a briefing on its website that stated: "While the current water, sanitation, and hygiene infrastructure in Haiti would certainly facilitate

Effects of a Warming World

Climate directly affects the incidence of waterborne illnesses through its effects on water temperature and the frequency and intensity of precipitation. According to many scientists, the earth is warming at an unnaturally rapid rate largely due to human activities. If this continues, they warn, it could lead to more severe storms, massive floods, and, inevitably, a higher prevalence of waterborne illness than exists today. The Union of Concerned Scientists writes:

> Extreme rainfall events have become more common in the United States at the same time the climate has warmed, and the problem will likely grow worse as the climate continues to warm, leaving more and more of our growing population vulnerable to the immediate and lingering health impacts of these events. While the risks of flooding to our homes and communities are based on a variety of factors, including where we live and how our region has developed, the influence of climate change can no longer be ignored.

Union of Concerned Scientists. *After the Storm: The Hidden Health Risks of Flooding in a Warming World,* March 2012. www.ucsusa.org/assets/documents /global_warming/climate-change-and-flooding.pdf.

transmission of cholera (and many other illnesses), cholera is not circulating in Haiti, and the risk of cholera introduction to Haiti is low."[29] The CDC's assumption proved to be wrong. The following October cholera was indeed discovered in Haiti, and it marked the beginning of a terrifying epidemic.

At first everyone was baffled by cholera's sudden appearance. It was not detected until nine months after the earthquake struck, which meant that it could not have been directly related to the quake. Since the illness had never affected people in Haiti before, observers wondered why it had suddenly appeared and where it had come from. The mystery was solved after an in-depth investigation led by Renaud Piarroux, a French physician who is an expert on infectious diseases. Piarroux's team found that the disease had originated at a United Nations camp in the mountains of central Haiti, where hundreds of Nepalese soldiers were staying.

The soldiers had arrived in Haiti on October 8, 2010, to help with the United Nations peacekeeping mission. Cholera had broken out in Nepal before they had left their homeland, and Piarroux concluded that some of the troops were carriers of the illness without being aware of it. This theory was strengthened after tests showed that the strain of cholera in Nepal was the exact same strain that affected Haiti. The investigation found that through careless sanitation practices, sewage containing infected fecal material had spilled on the grounds of the camp and was washed into a nearby stream during a rainstorm. Like all bacteria, once the *Vibrio cholerae* were in the water, they began to grow and multiply rapidly. Says Paul S. Keim, an infectious disease expert from Arizona: "It was like throwing a lighted match into a gasoline-filled room."[30]

Carried along by the current, the deadly pathogens flowed from the stream into Haiti's longest river, the Artibonite. From there they swept through the remaining waterways, spreading contamination throughout all the country's streams and rivers. The Haitian people regularly used these bodies of water for drinking, bathing, cooking, irrigating rice crops, and even brushing their teeth. They had no way of knowing that the water they depended on for their livelihoods could now kill them. One of these unsuspecting people was Jean Salgadeau Pelette, a thirty-eight-year-old man from the town of Mirebalais who regularly bathed in the Latem River. On October 16, 2010, Pelette's family members found him collapsed on the river-bank, sick and weakened from a sudden onset of violent stomach illness. They carried him home because he was too weak to walk, and by four o'clock that afternoon he was dead—the first victim of the deadly cholera outbreak that would soon spread to every Haitian province.

"So Sudden and So Brutal"

Within days of Pelette's death, hundreds of other people throughout the country were getting sick and dying from the vicious disease. On the afternoon of October 19, three children from the coastal town of Saint-Marc developed severe watery diarrhea while at school and died in their classroom. The following day the Saint Nicolas Hospital in Saint-Marc was overflowing with hundreds of desperately ill patients. They were doubled and tripled up in beds, lying on the floor in hallways, and even sprawled on the sidewalks outside. By that evening forty-four of the patients had died. "At that moment," says hospital director Yfto Mayette, "I felt like I didn't want to live any longer myself. It was so sudden and so brutal."[31] By early January 2011, just three months after the contamination at the United Nations camp, cholera had killed more than thirty-six hundred people in Haiti and sickened tens of thousands more.

Cholera continued to ravage Haiti for the rest of that year and into 2012 and showed no signs of ending. This was largely because severe water shortages persisted in many areas of the country, and people had no choice but to drink and bathe in contaminated water. An April 2012 investigative report by NPR found that despite the risks involved, most Haitians were still getting their water from rivers and streams. This was extremely disturbing to humanitarian workers such as Kenny Rae, who is with the human rights organization Oxfam International: "It's a tragedy," he says, "particularly in the middle of

Members of the Haitian Ministry of Health collect the bodies of cholera victims in Haiti. As of July 2012, over a half-million people had fallen ill from cholera, and the death toll had climbed past seventy-five hundred.

a cholera outbreak, when people have to use water they take from the river. We've tested it. It's very, very contaminated."[32] According to statistics posted online by the Haitian government, as of mid-July 2012 more than a half-million people had fallen ill from cholera, and the death toll had climbed past seventy-five hundred. The lingering fear among health officials, international aid groups, and the people of Haiti is that the country will never be completely rid of the illness that it had always managed to avoid in the past.

"The Worst Flooding in Living Memory"

In tropical countries like Haiti, outbreaks of cholera and other waterborne illnesses tend to be more severe during the summer months because that is the time of the monsoon. Monsoons, which occur between June and September each year, are seasonal wind shifts that influence climate and precipitation. With the monsoon comes rain—but not just normal rainstorms. These rains are such torrential downpours that they often result in extensive, widespread flooding. South Asia is well known for such severe floods because the region experiences some of the heaviest monsoon rains in the world. During the monsoon season of 2007, the South Asian countries of India, Bangladesh, and Nepal were hit with disastrous floods that UNICEF referred to as "the worst flooding in living memory."[33] For more than two weeks straight, heavy rains pounded the countries, flooding rivers, inundating massive swaths of land, and covering entire villages with up to 6 feet (1.83m) of water. Thousands of people were killed, and millions of others were left homeless after their houses or huts were swept away by raging floodwaters.

Because of the danger of water contamination, international aid groups warned that the area would become an ideal breeding ground for a serious outbreak of waterborne illness—and they were correct. Cholera broke out in the east Indian state of Orissa and killed an estimated 250 people. The state health secretary, Chinmoy Basu, said the illness was caused by people drinking from stagnant pools of water that had been contaminated during the flood. "Diarrhea is a seasonal problem," said Basu. "But in our case, the situation is severe."[34]

A Vulnerable Country

Of the South Asian countries that were affected by the 2007 flood, Bangladesh was hit the hardest. Often called the wettest country in the world, Bangladesh has more than seven hundred rivers and tributaries, as well as the world's largest delta formed by several major rivers. Because it is a low-lying country that is surrounded by water, Bangladesh is prone to severe flooding, especially during its monsoon season when pounding rainstorms overwhelm the capacity of the rivers— and when the floods come, the incidence of waterborne illness invariably soars. This was the case during the 2007 flood, when waterborne illness was rampant in Bangladesh. In August of that year, an estimated one hundred thousand people were admitted to hospitals for treatment, and more than half of the victims were suffering from diarrheal disease. In just one day more than four thousand patients were treated for diarrhea. A government health official stated: "The overall diarrhea situation is grim. Everyday there is a rush of patients. We are trying to cope with it."[35]

Under normal circumstances, the International Centre for Diarrhoeal Disease Research (often called the Cholera Hospital) in the Bangladeshi city of Dhaka saw about 150 patients each day. But in the aftermath of the 2007 flood, the number soared to more than 600 per day. The facility became so overrun with patients that workers erected a huge tent outside with bamboo poles and canvas sheeting. There was a desperate need for patient care, and hospital officials refused to turn anyone away who needed help. "At first," said a physician at the hospital, "it was mostly adult men who were probably drinking contaminated water at work. But in the last few days we've had an increase in the number of children, meaning that whole communities are now exposed to flood water and are getting sick."[36]

Bangladeshi villagers wade through floodwaters as they go to collect drinking water. In August 2007 over one hundred thousand people were admitted to hospitals, with the majority of cases being diarrhea.

The 2007 flood was just one of many crises that have afflicted Bangladesh over the years. The monsoon season of 2004, for instance, brought such severe flooding that two-thirds of the country was underwater. According to the humanitarian organization WaterAid, the 2004 flood was one of the worst ever seen in Bangladesh and "left havoc in its wake." The group explains: "Dhaka, the capital, was a city swimming in sewage. More than half the city was submerged in the weeks when the floodwaters began pouring, first from the swollen rivers as they burst their banks, then from over-burdened sewers disgorging back on to the street."[37] In the aftermath of the 2004 flood, Bangladesh was ravaged by waterborne illness. More than seventeen thousand people developed cholera, E. coli–related intestinal illnesses, and typhoid fever, and hundreds of them died.

A Deadly Outbreak in the Philippines

In September 2009, after back-to-back typhoons struck the Philippines, much of the country was submerged by a devastating flood. Within weeks a deadly waterborne illness known as leptospirosis had broken out in the capital city of Manila and several other regions. Leptospirosis is caused by contact with water that has been contaminated by the urine of rats, monkeys, and certain other animals. According to the WHO, leptospirosis bacteria commonly enter the body through cuts and abrasions on the skin. Symptoms include severe headaches, fever, and vomiting. In the most severe cases, sufferers can develop meningitis and bleeding of the lungs.

By mid-November 2009 nearly thirty-four hundred cases of leptospirosis infection were confirmed, and 249 people had died. In a report to the public, Philippines health secretary Francisco Duque stated: "There is a surge in the number of hospitalized cases

"A Humanitarian Crisis"

Pakistan experienced similar devastation during the summer of 2010. As in Bangladesh, waterborne illness is a continuous problem in Pakistan. Health officials estimate that 1.2 million lives are lost each year due to waterborne illnesses, including 250,000 children under age five who die from diarrheal disease. Says Pakistani physician Muhammad Ashraf Chaudhry: "The water-borne illnesses account for nearly 60% of child deaths in Pakistan with approximately 630 children dying daily from diarrhoea." Chaudhry adds that in some towns, at least 80 percent of the population drinks water that is contaminated because of improper treatment and storage. "Every day," he says, "nine out of ten times, the glass of water turns out to be 'unfit for human consumption' as the situation of public water sources, storage tanks, distribution channels etc. has become horrifying."[38]

of Leptospirosis from among the victims of recent typhoons who have [lost] . . . their homes. Various local government units and hospitals have reported an increasing number of cases of Leptospirosis among communities that have been submerged in flood waters and from among those who have been transferred to evacuation sites."

Quoted in IRIN Asia. "Philippines: Flood Victims Grapple with Leptospirosis," October 28, 2009. www.irinnews.org/Report/86779/PHILIPPINES-Flood-victims-grapple -with-Leptospirosi.

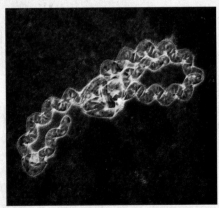

Infection with the leptospira bacterium (shown) is caused by contact with water that has been contaminated by the urine of rats, monkeys, and other animals.

These water contamination issues are worse during times of flooding, such as in July 2010. In the middle of the monsoon season, Pakistan experienced unusually heavy rains and was hit by the worst flooding it had seen in more than eighty years. "We have never seen such devastation in the past in Pakistan caused by floods, not in my lifetime,"[39] said International Medical Corps country director Jehangir Ali Khan. One-fifth of the country was completely submerged in floodwater—an area larger than England—and an estimated 8 million people lost their homes in the flood. While access to clean water has always been a problem in Pakistan, the floods significantly worsened the problem by breaking sewer lines open and filling wells with dirty water. Despite the fact that it was known to be contaminated, millions of people used the well water for drinking and bathing. They had no other choice because it was the only water available to them.

The Pakistani government and international aid groups worked frantically to get clean water to as many people as possible throughout the country. But the scale of the disaster

During Bangladesh's 2007 flooding, the International Centre for Diarrhoeal Disease Research's cholera hospital in Dhaka was overwhelmed with patients with diarrheal infections. The hospital was admitting six hundred people a day at the height of the flooding.

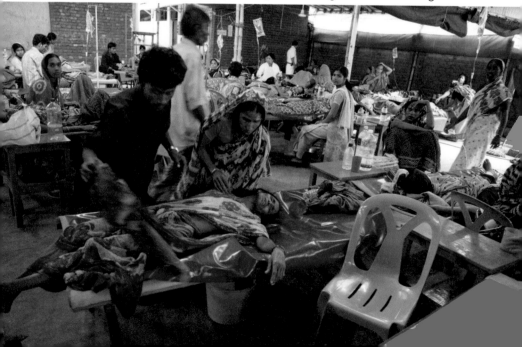

was so massive and so overwhelming that reaching everyone in need was impossible. In a September 2010 report to the U.S. Congress, Asian affairs specialists described the devastation in Pakistan, saying that the country was "in the midst of a catastrophic natural disaster that has precipitated a humanitarian crisis of major proportions." The authors went on to warn about the likelihood of a waterborne illness epidemic: "Little clean drinking water is available for many of the people who have been affected. Many of those, particularly children, are now in danger of disease outbreak, particularly diarrhea caused by ingesting stagnant water."[40]

Two little boys from the village of Pabbi were among those who became gravely ill after being exposed to contaminated floodwaters. Just before the flood destroyed the town, their father, Ikramullah Khan, abandoned his two-room house and all his possessions and fled to safety with his wife and four children. Shortly afterward his two sons, five-year-old Shahid and six-year-old Waqar, developed severe diarrhea and had to be rushed to the hospital. Ikramullah stood helplessly by them, sick with grief and terrified that after managing to escape the deadly flood and save his own life and the lives of his family, his precious sons could still die. "I saved my kids," he said. "That was everything for me. Now I see I'm losing them. We're devastated."[41] Ikramullah's despair was echoed by people throughout Pakistan whose lives were turned upside down by the catastrophic flood.

Inconceivable Pain and Misery

Wherever they strike, natural disasters such as earthquakes and floods cause destruction, devastation, and heartbreak. Once the disaster is over, the aftermath can intensify a terrible situation by leading to water contamination and severe shortages of clean, safe water—which means the spread of waterborne illness is inevitable. The greatest suffering is in the world's poorest developing countries, where these illnesses are already a severe problem. Cholera, diarrhea, and other life-threatening diseases can sweep through cities, towns, and villages and leave widespread sickness and death in their wake.

CHAPTER FIVE

How Waterborne Illnesses Are Treated

Medical science has produced an astounding array of treatments for human diseases and disorders. Thanks to advanced diagnostic techniques, sophisticated technology, and lifesaving drugs, scores of conditions that were once considered hopeless can now be prevented or cured. This is true of many waterborne illnesses, including typhoid fever and cholera. Years ago these diseases had exceptionally high fatality rates, whereas today patients who suffer from them can fully recover if treated in time. A major challenge, however, is for treatments to become more accessible to the developing world. That is where waterborne illnesses are most prevalent—and where a disturbing number of people, mostly children, die every day because they are not receiving the treatments they need.

A "Medical Miracle"

Of all the waterborne diseases that affect people in developing countries, those in the diarrheal category represent the most serious problem. If help can reach patients who need it most, these diseases are highly treatable because the primary characteristic—dehydration—can be remedied quickly. Without treatment, however, dehydration can be deadly. It occurs when a significant amount of the body's water has been lost, meaning that the amount of fluid leaving the body is greater than what is taken in. Water is an essential element of the human body; without adequate amounts the body cannot function properly. The sufferer's vital organs begin to fail, and he or she can die within a very short time. Thus, it is essential for rehydration treatment to begin at the first signs that someone has become dehydrated.

Although rehydration replaces lost fluids, it involves much more than feeding water to a patient. As the body loses large amounts of water, it is also depleted of essential nutrients such as electrolytes, which are mineral salts that are necessary for the body to function properly. To replenish these nutrients and to replace lost water, patients are treated with a solution known as oral rehydration salts, which is commonly referred to as ORS. This is a precise mixture of sugar, salt, and water that was invented by researchers at the International Centre

Children in India receiving oral hydration salts (ORS) to rehydrate. ORS is a precise measure of sugar, salt, and water and is used to rehydrate people who are dehydrated from diarrhea.

for Diarrhoeal Disease Research in Dhaka, Bangladesh. A 2009 report by UNICEF explains how ORS therapy works in children and why it is so effective in treating dehydration:

> In a healthy child, the small intestines absorb water and electrolytes from the digestive tract so that these nutrient-rich fluids may be transported to other parts of the body through the bloodstream. In a sick child, diarrhea-causing pathogens damage the intestines—causing an excessive amount of water and electrolytes to be secreted rather than being absorbed. When the ORS solution reaches the small intestines, the sodium and glucose in the mixture are transported together across the lining of the intestines, and the sodium, which is now in higher concentrations in the intestines, promotes water absorption back into the body from the [intestines].[42]

Because ORS therapy is so effective at curing dehydration, it is the primary treatment for people suffering from cholera—and it saves millions of lives every year. One person who has witnessed the results of this treatment is Josh Ruxin, a public health expert who founded and directs the humanitarian group Rwanda Works. In the early 1990s he visited a village in the South American country of Bolivia where cholera patients were being treated with ORS solution. Ruxin observed what he describes as a "medical miracle," as he writes: "A nearly lifeless child dehydrated by severe diarrhea was given sips of a sugar and salt solution and recovered in a couple of hours." Ruxin was amazed that such a simple treatment could save lives by quickly curing dehydration. Since that time he has seen how effective the treatment is at curing cholera patients of all ages, from tiny babies to adults. He feels strongly that measures must be taken for packets of ORS solution to be distributed throughout the world to everyone who needs them. He writes: "No one need die from this historic killer."[43]

Ruxin says that in southern Asia, ORS therapy has helped to reduce the cholera fatality rate from 30 percent to less than 1 percent. In the poverty-stricken African country of Rwanda,

"A Mystical Disease"

Seven-year-old Pierre Laban lives in a small village in Haiti called Savanne Ragé. One afternoon in March 2012 he suddenly began vomiting and was stricken with diarrhea. Immediately his grandmother began preparing traditional medicine from alcohol, plant roots, and dried leaves. But when Pierre's father, Pierre Osnel, arrived home he could see that the little boy was very weak and sick. "I felt that my son was dying," he says. "I thought that he had a mystical disease. But I also remembered that we recently had two people in the village that passed away after showing the same symptoms as Pierre." Osnel recalled that cholera was suspected in the two deaths, so he contacted community leaders, who arrived with a medical team. They gave the little boy oral rehydration solution and taught the family how to prepare it on their own. They also recommended that Pierre be taken to the hospital, where he could get better care.

By the time Osnel arrived at the hospital with his son, Pierre had become so weak and dehydrated that the staff administered intravenous solution. His condition improved quickly, and he was able to go home after two days. "My son . . . recovered very well," says Osnel. "Now I know that cholera happens, and it can be prevented and treated."

Quoted in United Nations Office for the Coordination of Humanitarian Affairs. "Haiti: Child Cured of 'Mystical Disease,'" May 10, 2012. www.unocha.org/top -stories/all-stories/haiti-child-cured-%E2%80%9Cmystical%E2%80%9D-disease.

where Ruxin lives, he witnessed a 2006 cholera outbreak that was "rapidly quelled" as six hundred community health workers "fanned out with oral rehydration packets in hand. Even a poor country has no excuse for letting people die from this disease."[44] Wherever ORS treatment has been used, the results are truly remarkable. Studies have shown that an estimated 80 percent of cholera sufferers can recover after prompt administration of oral rehydration therapy.

A More Aggressive Approach

For the sickest cholera patients, however, more intensive treatment is often necessary. Those who are suffering from severe dehydration may be too weak to drink ORS solution on their own, so they must be rehydrated intravenously. This involves rehydration fluids being injected into their veins, which is an essential lifesaving measure because it achieves rehydration so rapidly. Says Mark Pietroni, who directs the International Centre for Diarrhoeal Disease Research: "The biggest mistake is that patients do not get enough hydration fast enough. You have to give huge amounts of IV fluid in the first three hours—seven or eight liters. In Dhaka at the end of April you see people with IVs in each arm and leg. But as soon as the patient can drink, you switch them to oral rehydration."[45]

In addition to intravenous rehydration treatment, antibiotics are often prescribed for severely dehydrated cholera patients. These medications have been shown to lessen the severity of cholera symptoms while reducing the length of time patients suffer from diarrhea, which means they recover more quickly. Another benefit of antibiotics is that they significantly reduce the amount of *Vibrio cholerae* bacteria that are contained in feces. Thus, cholera patients stop shedding infectious organisms when they have bowel movements, which decreases the risk that they can pass the illness along to other people.

Hope for Typhoid Sufferers

Like cholera, typhoid is a diarrheal illness that carries the risk of dehydration, so patients may require prompt rehydration treatment. Along with watery diarrhea, typhoid symptoms also include high fever, abdominal pain, a headache that progressively grows worse, and overpowering fatigue. Based on these symptoms, a doctor may suspect typhoid and send the patient's stool sample to a laboratory so the diagnosis can be confirmed. Lab technicians use tests known as cultures to analyze the sample for pathogens, as the National Institutes of Health explains: "In the laboratory, a technician places a sample of the specimen in a special dish filled with a gel that encourages any bacteria or other germs that are present to grow. The culture is watched for growth. If there is growth, the germs are identified."[46] If no *Salmonella typhi* bacteria are detected by the lab technician, the doctor may order additional tests. Blood cultures, for instance, can detect bacteria in early phases of the illness when they might not show up in a patient's stool samples.

If the test confirms that the patient has typhoid, antibiotics are the primary treatment—and these medications have made a profound difference in people's ability to survive. Prior to the use of antibiotics, an estimated 20 percent of typhoid sufferers died, usually from infection, pneumonia, or intestinal bleeding. Since antibiotics have been widely used in typhoid treatment, the fatality rate has been reduced to 1 to 2 percent. The Regional Medical Center of San Jose, California, explains: "If typhoid is diagnosed and promptly treated with antibiotics, the outcome is usually good. But without treatment, fever and symptoms may continue for weeks or months, and death may occur as a result of complications from the bacterial infection."[47] Physicians have

Young typhoid fever patients receive treatment at a Philippine hospital. Typhoid symptoms include watery diarrhea, high fever, abdominal pain, progressively worsening headaches, and overpowering fatigue.

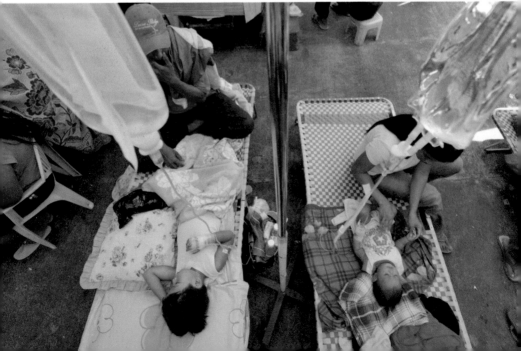

Dragon's Blood Treatment

Scientists have long searched for medicines to treat deadly diarrheal illnesses, which kill primarily through dehydration. In February 2011 they may have found what they were looking for when a research team completed a human trial of a new antidiarrheal drug known as crofelemer. It is derived from the sap of the *Croton lechleri* tree (also called Dragon's Blood), which is found in the northwestern Amazon basin of South America. Historically, *Croton lechleri* sap has been used by native tribes in South America to treat diarrhea. Scientists believed that a drug made from the sap could be effective in treating people with cholera, so they first tested it on animals. When it was shown to be effective in that experiment, the next step was to see how humans suffering from cholera responded to it.

The study was considered a great success. Crofelemer treatment reduced severe watery diarrhea among study participants while also balancing their fluid and electrolyte levels. Also, the drug was determined to be safe and had no serious side effects. The researchers plan to continue studies with crofelemer in more than one hundred developing countries where diarrheal diseases are the most serious problem.

The sap of the dragon's blood tree has been used for centuries by Amazon natives to reduce diarrhea symptoms.

numerous antibiotics from which to choose. They make choices for treating typhoid based on a number of factors, such as the geographic region where the patient contracted the illness. Typhoid strains from South America, for instance, are known to be resistant to certain varieties of antibiotics. If a particular kind of antibiotic is not effective for a patient, the doctor will prescribe another type and see if that works better.

In April 2011 a team of researchers from Vietnam and Nepal issued a joint statement about a new antibiotic called gatifloxacin, and they recommended that it be the primary drug for typhoid treatment. This conclusion was the result of a study that involved 884 children and adults who were typhoid patients. About half of the participants were given gatifloxacin. The remainder took an antibiotic called chloramphenicol, which has been the standard treatment for typhoid since the 1950s. The researchers found that both drugs were equally effective in terms of how patients responded to them, but the new drug offered significant advantages. Its dosage is once per day for seven days, compared with chloramphenicol's dosage of four times per day for fourteen days. This results in a significant cost savings, which is especially important in poor developing countries. Also, the patients in the study who took gatifloxacin had few side effects from the drug, whereas those who took chloramphenicol experienced nausea, diarrhea, and dizziness.

Counting on the Immune System

Although antibiotics can successfully treat typhoid, they do not necessarily work for other waterborne illnesses. Contrary to what is often believed, these medications are not miracle drugs that can cure everything—and in some cases, they do more harm than good. In people with E. coli infections, for example, antibiotics may encourage the growth of toxins in the intestines that cause diarrhea, which can lead to dehydration. In addition, antibiotics may increase the patient's risk for complications by encouraging the growth of harmful bacteria.

Antidiarrheal medications are also not recommended for people with E. coli infections even though bloody diarrhea is a primary symptom. These drugs help stop diarrhea by slowing down the rate at which food and waste products move through the intestines. For someone infected with E. coli, this allows more time for the body to absorb toxins produced by the bacteria. Thus, the medications can increase the risk of developing medical conditions such as blood disease and kidney problems.

Because of these complications, E. coli–related illnesses are among those for which there are no effective treatments. As frustrating as it can be for patients who feel miserable and are anxious to be cured, doctors cannot do much except recommend that they rest in bed and drink plenty of fluids. One of these illnesses is E. coli enteritis, which is an inflammation of the intestines caused by infection with E. coli bacteria. Along with bloody, mucus-filled diarrhea, symptoms include stomach cramps, loss of appetite, fever, nausea, exhaustion, and muscle aches. Because these symptoms resemble a common stomach virus (often referred to as stomach "flu"), a doctor will not necessarily suspect that the patient has been infected with E. coli. If there is reason for suspicion, a stool sample from the patient will be sent to a laboratory for examination. But even if the test is positive for the bacteria, the recommended treatment will likely still be limited to bed rest and fluids.

This is true of all E. coli infections, including the dangerous strain known as O157:H7. Symptoms, which are usually more severe than for other types of E. coli infection, include painful abdominal cramps and diarrhea that is frequent and extremely bloody. Because the illness is not treatable, little can be done for the patient except to wait for the immune system to fight off the infection—and in some cases, the body is unable to do that. The risks are especially high for the elderly, who often have weak immune systems, and children under age five, whose immune systems are not fully developed. If they are infected with E. coli O157:H7, the risks include acute kidney failure and damage to other vital organs such as the brain. One potential complication is the development of a life-threatening condition known as hemolytic uremic syndrome (HUS).

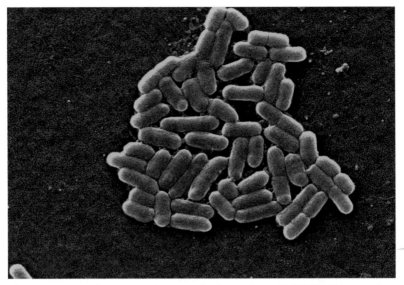

This scanning electron micrograph shows E. coli O157:H7 bacteria. This bacterium is one of the most dangerous strains, causing painful abdominal cramps and frequent, bloody diarrhea.

HUS, which is characterized by the destruction of red blood cells, is the primary cause of kidney failure in children. Many patients with this illness are hospitalized in intensive care units so medical staff can keep a close eye on their condition. They often receive blood transfusions and/or dialysis, which filters waste products from the blood. This was the case with two children who were infected with E. coli O157:H7 in October 2008. A five-year-old boy and seven-year-old girl were treated at the University of Iowa Children's Hospital after battling severe complications from the infection for more than a month. Both children developed HUS while staying at the hospital and were closely monitored by medical staff. After undergoing lifesaving treatments such as blood transfusions and kidney dialysis, the boy and girl were both expected to make a full recovery.

Worm Killer

Parasitic waterborne illnesses may also lead to life-threatening illnesses if they are not caught and treated early enough. Advanced cases of schistosomiasis, for instance, can lead to bacterial infections, abdominal bloating, urinary inflammation, and other problems, such as vaginal bleeding in females. Often individuals will not realize they have been infected until these symptoms are present. For instance, one woman who was infected by schistosoma parasites while swimming in a pond in Africa developed symptoms five months later and was convinced that she had some form of cancer. A physician who was examining a vaginal smear under a microscope was taken aback when he found worm eggs on the slide. Further testing confirmed that the woman did not have cancer but had developed complications from schistosomiasis.

The primary treatment for this parasitic disease is a drug called praziquantel. It is a strong medication that is given in one dose and works by disintegrating the worms that have infested a patient's bloodstream. Once the worms have been killed, they are flushed out of the body during bowel movements. The human rights organization the Carter Center, which

Former U.S. president Jimmy Carter (center) and former first lady Rosalyn Carter (on his right) pass out praziquantel pills to Nigerian children. President Carter refers to praziquantel as "one of the great miracle medical discoveries of the 1980s."

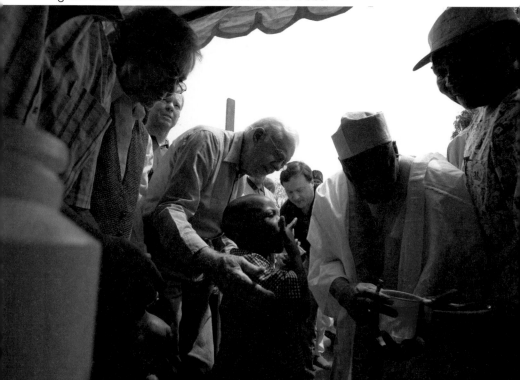

was founded by former U.S. president Jimmy Carter, refers to praziquantel as "one of the great miracle medical discoveries of the 1980s."[48] The center states that within six months of receiving a dose of praziquantel, up to 90 percent of the damage from schistosomiasis infection can be reversed.

Yet as effective as praziquantel has proved to be in the treatment of schistosomiasis, it is not accessible to many people in developing countries where the need is greatest. According to the WHO, less than 14 percent of people who require treatment are able to receive the drug, largely because they cannot afford it. This is especially true in sub-Saharan Africa and was the focus of an August 2010 article in the British journal the *Lancet*. The authors of the article, who are infectious disease specialists from the United States and Europe, refer to schistosomiasis as "one of the most devastating neglected tropical diseases." They urge global health organizations and drug manufacturers to collectively address the shortage of praziquantel, saying that widespread availability would prevent 280,000 deaths of school-age children each year. The authors write: "Praziquantel is urgently needed for sub-Saharan Africa now. . . . The shortages of praziquantel should be treated as an African humanitarian crisis."[49]

Progress and Challenges

Waterborne illnesses continue to be a major problem throughout the world, especially in the poorest developing countries. Many of these illnesses can be successfully treated, and millions of people who suffer from them can fully recover. That is only possible, however, if they have access to lifesaving medicines and treatments—and in a disturbing number of cases, they do not. International aid organizations such as UNICEF, along with numerous humanitarian groups, are working diligently to make treatments more accessible to those who need them most.

CHAPTER SIX

Global Efforts to Prevent Waterborne Illness

If there is one philosophy that is shared by doctors, nurses, health officials, and humanitarian organizations worldwide, it is that the only real solution to eliminating waterborne illnesses is preventing them—and that is an extraordinary undertaking. In developing countries, where these illnesses sicken and kill millions of people each year, the combination of water shortages and poor sanitation is an enormous, persistent problem. This is complicated by a lack of awareness: People often do not understand the connection between disease and human actions that contaminate water. Despite the challenges that remain, however, progress is being made. This is made possible due to the efforts of humanitarian groups and thousands of dedicated individuals who are committed to making a positive difference in the lives of people throughout the world.

"A Vital Step"

Because the need is so great, the United Nations and the WHO have declared access to safe drinking water to be among their highest priorities. A concerted effort toward accomplishing this goal began in September 2000 at the Millennium Summit, which was the largest gathering of world leaders in history. One outcome of the summit was the adoption of Millennium Development Goals, which address such crucial global issues as extreme poverty and hunger, child mortality, disease, gender equality, and environmental sustainability, among others. A major priority identified at the gathering was to reduce by half the number of people worldwide who do not have access to safe drinking water by the year 2015.

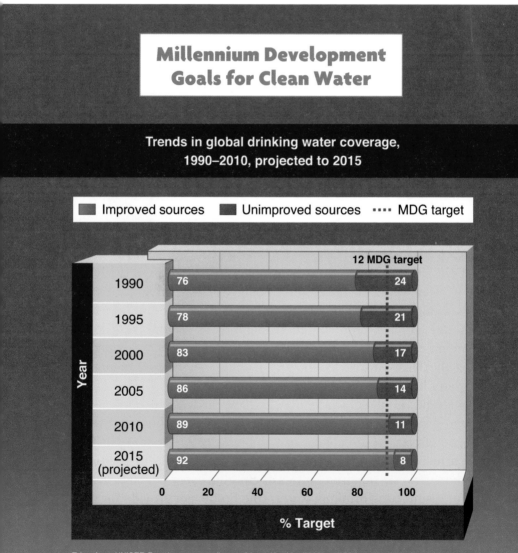

Millennium Development Goals for Clean Water

Trends in global drinking water coverage, 1990–2010, projected to 2015

■ Improved sources   ■ Unimproved sources   ···· MDG target

Year	Improved sources	Unimproved sources
1990	76	24
1995	78	21
2000	83	17
2005	86	14
2010	89	11
2015 (projected)	92	8

12 MDG target

% Target

According to a March 2012 UNICEF report, this goal was achieved five years ahead of schedule. In 2010, 11 percent of the global population did not have access to improved drinking water sources, meaning supplies of freshwater that were protected from contaminants. This was a significant improvement over 24 percent in 1990. Says United Nations secretary-general Ban Ki-moon: "Since 1990, more than 2 billion people have gained access to improved drinking water sources. This achievement is a testament to the commitment of Government leaders, public and private sector entities, communities and individuals who saw the target not as a dream, but as a vital step towards improving health and well-being."[50]

Yet even though the situation has markedly improved, nearly 800 million people still do not have access to clean, safe drinking water. Also, progress toward the clean water goal was based on averages, meaning that it does not apply to all countries. For example, more than 90 percent of people in North Africa, Latin America, the Caribbean, and large parts of Asia now have access to improved water sources, compared with only 61 percent in sub-Saharan Africa. Much work remains to be done, as waterborne illnesses can only be prevented in the developing world if access to clean water sources is improved.

Global Quest for Clean Water

UNICEF has numerous strategies in place to address the lack of clean water in developing countries. The organization is working in more than ninety countries worldwide to improve water supplies and sanitation facilities in schools and communities and to promote safe hygiene practices. One example is the West African country of Guinea, where contaminated water has led to regular outbreaks of waterborne illness. After widespread cholera infection in 2009, UNICEF worked with the government and international aid groups to boost prevention efforts. In the village of Kambaya, for instance, UNICEF partnered with a local group known as Tinkisso to produce more than six hundred bottles of chlorine every day to be used for disinfecting drinking water. One bottle can provide for the

Yemeni women fill plastic cans with water from a United Nations clean water tank. UNICEF has worked with governments and international aid groups to get clean water to people around the world.

needs of a family for one month and contributes significantly to improved hygiene and health. The bottles of chlorine solution, known as Sur'Eau, are sold for a modest price at community retail centers, and this has led to widespread use of chlorine throughout Kambaya. Says a resident named Sefanta, who is the mother of four children: "Since we started using chlorine in the village, children stopped complaining about their belly, and my children have no more [diarrhea]. You just have to drop the contents of the cork in a 20-liter bucket full of water, and it's decontaminated."[51]

These and other efforts have markedly decreased the incidence of waterborne illness in Kambaya and other communities throughout Guinea. According to a 2012 UNICEF report, prior to 2007 more than eight thousand cases of cholera were reported annually in the country. As a result of chlorination programs and promotion of better sanitation, Guinea has seen a 77 percent decrease in the rates of diarrhea and other waterborne illness— and in 2010 there were no cases of cholera at all.

Similar progress has been made in other parts of the world because of the efforts of UNICEF and other humanitarian

Help from the Air

In tropical regions of the world, the parasitic waterborne illness schistosomiasis is a devastating problem, and it sickens and kills hundreds of thousands of people every year. Those who live in isolated areas are often not aware of the illness or its symptoms, nor do they know how easily it can be contracted. A humanitarian group called Medicine on the Move, which is based in the West African country of Ghana, is making an effort to change that. The group trains women to be health-care workers and also to build and pilot small airplanes. Each week, the women fly over isolated villages on Lake Volta, an enormous human-made lake that is known to be infested with the snails that harbor schistosoma parasites. The pilots drop packages of educational materials onto school playgrounds so that teachers will pick them up and distribute them. The materials educate people about how they catch schistosomiasis, how to prevent it, and how the illness is treated.

This effort, combined with the government's schistosomiasis prevention program, is making a significant difference in the awareness of waterborne illnesses among the Ghanaian people. In 2008, 12.4 million were treated for the illness, and by 2010 that number had nearly tripled.

The Ghanaian government, along with the humanitarian group Medicine on the Move, has been helping educate people along Lake Volta about schistosomiasis.

organizations. Oxfam International, for instance, is involved in numerous ongoing projects to make water safer for people to drink. In the hillside village of Font de Liane in Haiti, the Oxfam group is installing what they call chlorine boxes, which are green metal poles with dispensers on top. When someone taps the box, it squirts enough chlorine to disinfect a 5-gallon bucket (18.9L) of water. Oxfam's plan is to install ninety of the chlorine boxes in the surrounding villages, which now get their water from contaminated streams. The Haitian people are excited about the projects because they are personally involved in something that will cut down on disease. Says Jacob Labote, a schoolteacher who is chair of Font de Liane's water committee: "We were thirsty for something like this. I believe that everybody will be using it."[52]

The Tap Project

Another UNICEF endeavor is known as the Tap Project, which began in New York City with the theme "When You Take Water, Give Water." The idea behind the program is that people who eat in restaurants receive glasses of water at no charge but may be willing to pay for it if their money is donated to a worthy cause. So each year during World Water Week, patrons at hundreds of restaurants throughout the United States are asked if they will contribute one dollar for their water. They learn that four thousand children die every day from waterborne illness and that just one dollar will buy forty days of clean drinking water for a child in need. All monies collected go toward UNICEF's efforts to bring clean and accessible water to millions of children around the world. Since the Tap Project began in 2007, nearly $3 million has been raised to provide children with clean water.

A major reason the Tap Project has been so successful is the enormous support it has gotten from restaurant owners and patrons, as well as donors and volunteers. One well-known celebrity who is an ambassador for UNICEF and supports the Tap Project is Selena Gomez. She admits that before becoming involved with the program, clean water was not something she thought about very often; like many people in industrialized countries, she had a tendency to take clean water for granted. "I can turn on the faucet or shower at home, and out it comes," she says. "Sadly, this is not the case for millions of people around the world." Gomez has traveled extensively with UNICEF and has seen for herself the devastating effect that the lack of clean, safe water can have on children. "In fact," she says, "thousands of them die every day simply because they can't access this precious resource. Others do not have the chance to go to school because they spend hours walking each day to gather water for their families." Gomez believes that if people work together toward the goal of making clean drinking water accessible to children, such bleak realities could become a thing of the past. "Just a little goes a very long way," she says. "One dollar—less than the price of a cup of coffee—can provide a child with clean drinking water for 40 days."[53]

Actress Selena Gomez is an ambassador for UNICEF and uses her celebrity status to bring awareness to the importance of clean drinking water for everyone.

Teen on a Mission

Nineteen-year-old Joel Mwale is not a famous celebrity like Gomez, but to the people who live in his native country of Kenya, he is truly a shining star. In about 2007, Mwale had a vision for making clean drinking water more accessible to his village—and the vision took shape while he was deathly ill with dysentery. He developed the illness after drinking contaminated water that was distributed by the village council during the annual dry season. Even though Mwale was weak and sick, while lying in a hospital bed he began thinking about the many others in his village who had also been sick with dysentery. He was determined to figure out a way to make safe drinking water available to his neighbors. He told himself: "I should do something. I'm not just going to sit back and watch things happen."[54]

When Mwale was released from the hospital, he invested all the money he had to build a deep well known as a borehole in his village. This would allow groundwater to be tapped for the community water supply, so villagers would no longer need to rely on surface water that was likely contaminated. Mwale and a group of volunteers began to dig on a patch of farmland until they struck water. Then the team installed pipes and a mechanical system that would enable the water to be extracted from the ground. Says Mwale: "It works in such a way that somebody has just got to turn a wheel then a lot of water comes out on the other end."[55]

The borehole functioned exactly as Mwale had hoped. More than one hundred villagers began visiting the well each day to collect their water free of charge. Mwale was so encouraged that he started thinking about ways to furnish clean water to even larger groups of people. The answer came to him during a rainstorm, as he explains: "One day while I was walking around my community . . . it was raining and I saw water running off the ground. So I said that if there's anything that I can do to be able to trap this rain water, store it in a reservoir, then be able to purify it and sell it to the public . . . this can be a good idea."[56] The idea of harvesting rainwater led to the creation of a company that Mwale called Sky Drop Enterprise. Using money lent to him by a local farmer, he purchased equipment and set up his new business.

Today Sky Drop is a thriving company that collects rainwater and stores it in enormous tanks. The water is filtered and purified by ultraviolet rays from the sun and then bottled for sale. The company produces as much as ten thousand bottles of purified water per month and sells them to people throughout Kenya for about half the price of regular bottled water. This venture is one more way that Mwale is helping prevent waterborne illness by improving people's access to clean water.

Ending Waste, Saving Lives

Derreck Kayongo also works to prevent waterborne illness, but he does it in a different way—by providing people with soap. A former war refugee from the African country of Uganda, Kayongo had seen firsthand the health problems that were caused by the lack of soap. Before fleeing his native country for Kenya, Kayongo had spent time in a refugee camp. He saw how vulnerable families were to disease, including those that are waterborne, because they had no soap or clean water to use for washing their hands. He became inspired to help change this after staying at a hotel in the United States, where he noticed that barely used bars of soap were thrown away. Through some research he learned that in North America alone, this amounts to hundreds of millions of soap bars discarded by the hospitality industry each year. Says Kayongo: "I was shocked just to know how much (soap) at the end of the day was thrown away. . . . Are we really throwing away that much soap at the expense of other people who don't have anything? It just doesn't sound right."[57] Kayongo decided to undertake a venture that would cut down on the enormous waste while helping to provide much-needed soap to poor developing countries. In 2009 he and his wife founded an organization called the Global Soap Project.

Today Kayongo's organization works with more than nine hundred hotels throughout North America. All the soap that is

Derreck Kayongo displays the slightly used bars of soap he collects for his Global Soap Project. He has distributed more than 350,000 bars of soap in nearly two dozen countries.

collected is sent to a reprocessing location near Atlanta, Georgia. The soap is stripped, cleaned, reprocessed into new soap, and tested to make sure there is no trace of bacteria left. The bars are then cut into smaller pieces and shipped to regions of the world where people need it most. As of June 2012 the Global Soap Project had distributed more than 350,000 bars of soap to twenty-three countries, including Haiti, South Sudan, Benin, Guatemala, Honduras, and Afghanistan. Says Kayongo: "There is good in all of us banding together to solve a problem."[58]

The Walk of Shame

People all over the world are banding together to address ways of preventing waterborne illness, and their efforts are making a significant difference. One of the most pressing issues is unhygienic practices such as open defecation, since it is still common in many areas of the developing world. A major goal of UNICEF and other humanitarian groups is to convince people that the practice needs to stop because they are putting their health, and the health of their children, at risk. One example is the southeast African country of Malawi, where many people living in rural villages are accustomed to defecating openly. They have always relieved themselves that way and see no need for latrines.

One person who is determined to change that is a teenage girl named Maureen Mbewe, who lives in the Malawi village of Mkangeni. After becoming frustrated with what she saw as a disgusting practice, Mbewe joined a UNICEF-sponsored group that was made up of more than three hundred adults and children from her village. The group engages in what is called Community-Led Total Sanitation exercises. The goal of these exercises is for villages to shame those who practice open defecation so they will abandon the practice in favor of using latrines.

In much of Africa many people do not have latrines in or near their houses. UNICEF sponsors a group that shames those who practice open defecation so they will abandon the practice and thus lessen the spread of disease.

A Lifesaving Straw

To help address the dire need for clean drinking water in developing countries, a Swiss company created a portable water purification tool known as the LifeStraw. The device is made of plastic and resembles a flute, and it is designed to hang around someone's neck. As with a regular drinking straw, the individual simply puts the LifeStraw in water and sucks. As the water is pulled through filters, the device removes pathogenic bacteria and other disease-causing organisms. One LifeStraw can filter up to 185 gallons (700L) of water, which is the average amount one person drinks in a year.

The exercise begins with the group assembling to discuss and analyze their village's sanitation habits. They point out homes that have latrines and identify locations where people without latrines are known to relieve themselves. According to environmental health officer Thomas Mchimpa, the young people involved in the exercise are much more willing to disclose information about open defecation than adults. "We find that many adults are appalled by the idea of disclosing their sanitation habits," says Mchimpa, "but it's often the children that are forthcoming with information. They will point to a nearby bush or river after which we ask the community to lead us there."[59] The group goes on what is known as a walk of shame, whereby they walk together to the identified spot. A designated individual scoops up the excrement and places it in a plastic bag, then asks group members to guess how much it weighs. Participants are often astonished as well as disgusted when they discover how much human waste is lying in the open.

A walk of shame in Mkangeni led to astounding results. After the exercise was over, six people stepped forward to take responsibility for developing an action plan for the village. Mbewe was ecstatic. "We'll have fewer illnesses when we all

PeePoo Prevention

Anders Wilhelmson is a Swedish architect and professor who wanted to do something to help improve hygiene and prevent waterborne illness in developing countries. After study trips in Asia and Africa, Wilhelmson was dismayed at the number of people who flung bags of excrement on the ground. So he founded a company called PeePoople and invented a disposable bag called the PeePoo. It looks like a normal plastic bag but is actually a single-use biodegradable "toilet." After using the bag, the person knots it and then buries it. A lining of special crystals in the bag sterilizes the waste and then breaks it down into fertilizer for crops.

In June 2012 Wilhelmson received a prestigious humanitarian award for his PeePoo invention. In presenting the award, a spokesperson said: "To be able to go to the toilet in a safe and secure manner is perhaps natural for many of us, however in many parts of the world this is not the case. More than 2.6 billion people lack access to basic sanitation today. . . . The invention of the self-sanitising Peepoo toilet has given an increased security to already vulnerable people and also has a significantly positive impact on the environment."

Quoted in Martina Nee. "Peepoo Inventor Professor Anders Wilhelmson Receives Top Honors in Änglamarkspriset 2012." Sting Capital, June 19, 2012. www.sting capital.com/SV/122/peepoople-anglamark.

Swedish architect and professor Anders Wilhelmson invented a disposable waste bag, the PeePoo bag, a single-use biodegradable "toilet" that afterward turns human feces into fertilizer.

have pit latrines," she says. "I want to see every home own one. My job from now on will be to encourage my friends who don't have a latrine to pressure their parents to build one."[60] This effort has resulted in significant achievements throughout Malawi. Hundreds of villages have been declared free of open defecation, and cholera cases have dramatically declined.

Ongoing Efforts

From chlorinating water and furnishing soap to countries in need to programs that end open defecation, organizations and individuals throughout the world are making strides toward preventing waterborne illness. As these efforts continue and new ones are undertaken, the time may eventually come when millions of people no longer have to suffer and die because of the dangerous effects of unsafe water.

Notes

Introduction: When Water Sickens and Kills

1. Ban Ki-moon. "Secretary-General's Message on World Water Day." United Nations, March 22, 2010. www.un.org/sg /statements/?nid=4446.
2. Centers for Disease Control and Prevention. "Chapter 8: Rural Water Supplies and Water-Quality Issues." *Healthy Housing Reference Manual*, December 8, 2009. www.cdc .gov/nceh/publications/books/housing/cha08.htm.

Chapter One: What Are Waterborne Illnesses?

3. American Academy of Microbiology. *E. Coli: Good, Bad, & Deadly*. 2011. http://academy.asm.org/images/stories /documents/EColi.pdf.
4. Quoted in Erin Toner. "The Legacy of Milwaukee's Crypto Outbreak 15 Years Ago." WUWM, October 8, 2008. www .wuwm.com/news/wuwm_news.php?articleid=3793.
5. International Association for Medical Assistance to Travelers. *Be Aware of Schistosomiasis*, 2010. www.iamat.org /pdf/be_aware_of_schistosomiasis.pdf.
6. Quoted in Richard Knox. "In Haiti, Bureaucratic Delays Stall Mass Cholera Vaccinations." NPR, March 27, 2012. www.npr.org/blogs/health/2012/03/27/149403215/in-haiti -bureaucratic-delays-stall-mass-cholera-vaccinations.
7. Indigo. Comment on Jerry R. Balentine. "Typhoid Fever." MedicineNet, June 15, 2011. www.medicinenet.com /typhoid_fever/article.htm.

Chapter Two: The Consequences of Human Actions

8. Quoted in Zachary Ochieng. "Kenya Family Stricken After Drinking Foul Water." OneWater, 2010. www.onewater

.org/stories/story/kenya_family_stricken_after_drinking
_foul_water.

9. Quoted in Meera Delal. "Cholera in Haiti: From Control to
Elimination." Al Jazeera, January 13, 2012. www.aljazeera
.com/indepth/features/2012/01/2012111193155842439.html.

10. Rose George. *The Big Necessity: The Unmentionable
World of Human Waste and Why It Matters.* New York:
Metropolitan, 2008, p. 2.

11. Plan Pakistan. "Ending Open Defecation in Rural Pakistan," January 2012. http://plan-international.org/where-we
-work/asia/pakistan/what-we-do/our-successes/ending-open
-defecation-in-rural-pakistan.

12. Jane Bean. "Rivers of Death: Tackling the Water and Sanitation Problems in Bangladesh." Australian Aid, July 9,
2012. http://ausaid.govspace.gov.au/2012/07/09/rivers-of
-death-tackling-the-water-and-sanitation-problems-in
-bangladesh.

13. Quoted in Adelaide Lusambili. *Flying Toilets.* Economic
& Social Research Council, 2011. http://steps-centre.org
/wpsite/wp-content/uploads/Flying_Toilets1.pdf.

14. Quoted in Lusambili, *Flying Toilets.*

15. Natural Resources Defense Council. "Facts About Pollution from Livestock Farms." January 13, 2011. www.nrdc
.org/water/pollution/ffarms.asp.

16. David Barstow. "A Deadly Germ Taints a Tradition: E. Coli
Devastates Families and Leaves a Fair in Doubt." *New York
Times,* September 20, 1999. www.nytimes.com/1999/09/20
/nyregion/deadly-germ-taints-tradition-e-coli-devastates
-families-leaves-fair-doubt.html?pagewanted=all&src=pm.

Chapter Three: Where Human Suffering Is Greatest

17. Robert D. Morris. *The Blue Death: Disease, Disaster, and
the Water We Drink.* New York: HarperCollins, 2007, p. 1.

18. UNICEF. *Diarrhoea: Why Children Are Still Dying and
What Can Be Done,* 2009. www.unicef.org/media/files
/Final_Diarrhoea_Report_October_2009_final.pdf.

19. Quoted in Jajati Karan. "Orissa in Grip of Cholera; Toll
Rises to 140." CNN-IBN, September 13, 2010. http://ibnlive

.in.com/news/orissa-in-grip-of-cholera-toll-rises-to-38
/130840-3.html.

20. Quoted in Rachel Dwyer. "Zimbabwe Appeal: First Cholera. Now It's Malaria and Anthrax." *Mashonaland West:
Did You Know* (blog), December 7, 2008. http://rainbow
warrior2005.wordpress.com/tag/mashonaland-west.

21. Quoted in IRIN Africa. "Zimbabwe: Growing Risk of Waterborne Diseases in Rural Areas," January 3, 2012. www
.irinnews.org/Report/94575/ZIMBABWE-Growing-risk-of
-waterborne-diseases-in-rural-areas.

22. Melissa Burns. "Lifesaving Drug Praziquantel Too Expen-
sive for Africa." *Pacific Standard*, October 3, 2010. www
.psmag.com/health/lifesaving-drug-praziquantel-too-expen
sive-for-africa-23538.

23. Medicine on the Move. "Medicine on the Move (MoM) Im-
proves Lives of West Africans Through Community-Based
Healthcare Education." www.medicineonthemove.org.

24. Quoted in IRIN Africa. "Health: Airdrops to Fight Schistosomiasis in Ghana," May 15, 2012. www.irinnews.org
/report/95450/HEALTH-Airdrops-to-fight-schistosomiasis
-in-Ghana.

25. Quoted in *SunStar Cebu* (Cebu City, Philippines). "Residents Almost 100% Affected by Schistosomiasis," June 11,
2012. www.sunstar.com.ph/tacloban/local-news/2012/06
/11/residents-almost-100-affected-schistosomiasis-226263.

26. Quoted in Jeffrey Bigongiari. "Polio Cases on the Rise in
Afghanistan, Pakistan." *Vaccine News Daily*, July 5, 2012.
http://vaccinenewsdaily.com/asia/319262-polio-cases-on
-the-rise-in-afghanistan-pakistan.

27. Quoted in BBC News. "Bangladesh Begins New Polio
Drive," March 2, 2007. http://news.bbc.co.uk/2/hi/south
_asia/6412835.stm.

Chapter Four: Waterborne Illness Catastrophes

28. Quoted in UN News Centre. "UN Warns on Waterborne
Disease Risk Among Flood-Affected Pakistanis," August
16, 2010. www.un.org/apps/news/story.asp?NewsID=3563
4&Cr=pakistan&Cr1.

29. Centers for Disease Control and Prevention. "Acute Watery Diarrhea and Cholera: Haiti Pre-decision Brief for Public Health Action," March 2, 2010. http://emergency .cdc.gov/disasters/earthquakes/haiti/waterydiarrhea_pre -decision_brief.asp.

30. Quoted in Deborah Sontag. "In Haiti, Global Failures on a Cholera Epidemic." *New York Times*, March 31, 2012. www.nytimes.com/2012/04/01/world/americas/haitis -cholera-outraced-the-experts-and-tainted-the-un.html ?pagewanted=all.

31. Quoted in Sontag. "In Haiti, Global Failures on a Cholera Epidemic."

32. Quoted in Richard Knox. "Water in the Time of Cholera: Haiti's Most Urgent Health Problem." NPR, April 12, 2012. www.npr.org/blogs/health/2012/04/13/150302830/water-in -the-time-of-cholera-haitis-most-urgent-health-problem.

33. UNICEF. "Millions of People Across South Asia Affected by Monsoonal Flooding," August 3, 2007. www.unicef.org /media/media_40495.html.

34. Quoted in K.S. Elias. "Disease Outbreak Strikes Thousands in Flood-Hit East India." *Gospel Herald*, September 4, 2007. www.gospelherald.net/article/mcat/43853/disease -outbreak-strikes-thousands-in-flood-hit-east-india.htm# .UB5Wd6Dh-So.

35. Quoted in Serajul Islam Quadir. "Bangladesh Flood Death Toll Nears 500." Reuters. www.reuters.com/article /2007/08/15/environment-bangladesh-floods-dc-idUSDHA 3025220070815.

36. Quoted in John Sudworth. "Disease Stalks Bangladesh Flood Victims." BBC News, August 9, 2007. http://news .bbc.co.uk/2/hi/south_asia/6939150.stm.

37. WaterAid. "Aftermath of the 2004 Bangladesh Flood," 2011. www.wateraid.org/uk/what_we_do/where_we_work /bangladesh/436.asp#.

38. Quoted in Pakistan Water Gateway. "Twin Cities: Water-Borne Diseases on the Rise?," August 11, 2011. http://water info.net.pk/cms/?q=node/128.

39. Quoted in Margaret Aguirre. "International Medical Corps Establishes Waterborne Disease Treatment Center at Pakistan Hospital." ReliefWeb, August 25, 2010.

http://reliefweb.int/report/pakistan/international-medical
-corps-establishes-waterborne-disease-treatment-center
-pakistan.

40. K. Alan Kronstadt, Pervaze A. Sheikh, and Bruce Vaughn.
*Flooding in Pakistan: Overview and Issues for Con-
gress.* CRS Report for Congress, September 21, 2010.
http://fpc.state.gov/documents/organization/150191.pdf.

41. Quoted in Asif Shahzad. "Waterborne Disease a Threat
for Pakistan's Children." *Huffington Post,* August 29,
2010. www.huffingtonpost.com/2010/08/29/waterborne
-disease-a-thre_n_698334.html.

Chapter Five: How Waterborne Illnesses Are Treated

42. UNICEF. *Diarrhoea.*

43. Josh Ruxin. "A Sugar and Salt Solution for Haiti's Cholera
Epidemic." *On the Ground* (blog), *New York Times,*
November 5, 2010. http://kristof.blogs.nytimes.com/2010
/11/05/a-sugar-and-salt-solution-for-haitis-cholera-epidemic.

44. Ruxin. "A Sugar and Salt Solution for Haiti's Cholera
Epidemic."

45. Quoted in Tina Rosenberg. "Saving Lives in a Time of
Cholera." *Opinionator* (blog), *New York Times,* April 7,
2012. http://opinionator.blogs.nytimes.com/2012/04/07
/saving-lives-in-a-time-of-cholera.

46. National Institutes of Health. "Fecal Culture," April 26,
2012. www.nlm.nih.gov/medlineplus/ency/article/003758
.htm.

47. Regional Medical Center of San Jose. "Typhoid Vaccine,"
December 30, 2011. http://regionalmedicalsanjose.com
/your-health/index.dot?id=187054&lang=English&db=hlt
&ebscoType=healthindex&widgetTitle=EBSCO%20Health
%20Library%20Index.

48. Carter Center. "Schistosomiasis Control Program," 2007.
http://eid.ac.cn/MirrorResources/5090.

49. Peter J. Hotez, Dirk Engels, Alan Fenwick, and Lorenzo
Savioli. "Africa Is Desperate for Praziquantel." *Lancet,*
August 2010. www.thelancet.com/journals/lancet/article
/PIIS0140673610608793/fulltext?_eventId=login&rss=yes.

Chapter Six: Global Efforts to Prevent Waterborne Illness

50. Quoted in UNICEF and World Health Organization. *Progress on Drinking Water and Sanitation*, March 2012. www.unicef.org/media/files/JMPreport2012.pdf.

51. Quoted in UNICEF. "At a Glance: Guinea," March 19, 2010. www.unicef.org/infobycountry/guinea_53091.html.

52. Quoted in Knox. "Water in the Time of Cholera."

53. Selena Gomez. "UNICEF Tap Project 2012." Field Notes, March 16, 2012. http://fieldnotes.unicefusa.org/2012/03 /selena-gomez-unicef-tap-project-2012.html?utm_source =feedburner&utm_medium=feed&utm_campaign=Feed %3A+unicefusa%2Ffieldnotes+%28UNICEF+USA+Field notes%29.

54. Quoted in Robyn Curnow. "How Falling Ill with Dysentery Inspired a Kenyan Teenager." CNN, November 14, 2011. http://edition.cnn.com/2011/11/14/business/skydrop -kenya-water/index.html.

55. Quoted in Curnow. "How Falling Ill with Dysentery Inspired a Kenyan Teenager."

56. Quoted in Curnow. "How Falling Ill with Dysentery Inspired a Kenyan Teenager."

57. Quoted in Ashley Fantz. "Lack of Soap Means Illness, Death for Millions of Children." CNN, November 15, 2011. www.cnn.com/2011/11/15/health/cnnheroes-soap-hygiene /index.html.

58. Quoted in Cara Hetland. "Global Soap Project." South Dakota Public Broadcasting, October 15, 2010. www.sdpb .org/tv/shows.aspx?MediaID=58649&Parmtype=RADIO &ParmAccessLevel=sdpb-all.

59. Quoted in Victor Chinyama. "Changing Sanitation Habits Through a 'Walk of Shame.'" UNICEF, October 26, 2010. www.unicef.org/malawi/reallives_6957.html.

60. Quoted in Chinyama. "Changing Sanitation Habits Through a 'Walk of Shame.'"

Glossary

dehydration: An excessive loss of bodily fluids and essential nutrients, often due to diarrhea.

diarrheal disease: An umbrella term that refers to a group of illnesses of which diarrhea (frequent liquid bowel movements) is the primary symptom.

electrolytes: Essential minerals such as sodium, potassium, and chloride.

feces: Human or animal waste (also known as stool or excrement).

host: An organism that provides an environment for a virus or parasite to grow and thrive.

monsoon: Seasonal wind shifts that influence climate and precipitation and are typically accompanied by extremely heavy rain and flooding.

neglected tropical diseases: Diseases that are confined to tropical regions of the world, such as South America, Africa, Asia, and the Middle East.

pathogen: A disease-causing organism.

runoff: What occurs when rain or melted snow cannot be absorbed and held by the soil, so the water runs over the ground and washes into surface water such as streams, rivers, and lakes.

strain: A term scientists use when referring to types or varieties of organisms, such as types of bacteria or viruses.

Organizations to Contact

Blue Planet Network

PO Box 3059
Redwood City, CA 94064-3059
Phone: (415) 762-4340
Website: http://blueplanetnetwork.org

The Blue Planet Network seeks to increase the impact of safe drinking water and sanitation programs for people throughout the world. Its website offers facts and statistics, photos and essays about the world's water crisis, and information about the countries that have the greatest needs.

Centers for Disease Control and Prevention (CDC)

1600 Clifton Rd.
Atlanta, GA 30333
Phone: (800) 232-4636
Website: www.cdc.gov

An agency of the U.S. Department of Health and Human Services, the CDC seeks to promote health and quality of life by controlling disease, injury, and disability. Its website offers numerous articles about waterborne illness, which can be accessed through its search engine.

Natural Resources Defense Council (NRDC)

40 W. Twentieth St.
New York, NY 10011
Phone: (212) 727-2700 • fax: (212) 727-1773
Website: www.nrdc.org

The NRDC is an environmental action group that works to protect the environment, humans, and wildlife. Numerous fact sheets, articles, and reports can be accessed through its website's search engine.

Operation Blessing International

977 Centerville Turnpike
Virginia Beach, VA 23463
Phone: (757) 226-3440 • fax: (757) 226-3657
Website: www.ob.org

Operation Blessing is a faith-based humanitarian organization that provides disaster relief, medical aid, hunger relief, clean water, and community development in more than twenty countries throughout the world. Its website offers numerous articles about waterborne illness and the work the organization does to help prevent it.

Oxfam International

1100 Fifteenth St. NW, Suite 600
Washington, DC 20005
Phone: (202) 496-1170 • fax: (202) 496-0128
Website: www.oxfam.org

Oxfam is a humanitarian organization that seeks to fight poverty throughout the world and provide assistance to people who are affected by natural disasters or conflict. Its website offers a number of publications about waterborne illness, including news releases about how Oxfam helps people who are in need.

Pacific Institute

654 Thirteenth St.
Preservation Park
Oakland, CA 94612
Phone: (510) 251-1600 • fax: (510) 251-2203
Website: www.pacinst.org

The Pacific Institute is dedicated to finding solutions to water shortages, habitat destruction, global warming, and environmental injustice. Its website offers reports, research, testimonials, opinion pieces, and a search engine that produces a number of articles about waterborne illness.

United Nations Children's Fund (UNICEF)

3 United Nations Plaza
New York, NY 10017
Phone: (212) 326-7000; (212) 779-1679
Website: www.unicef.org

UNICEF works in 190 countries and territories to help children survive and thrive from early childhood through adolescence. A wealth of information about water, sanitation, and waterborne illness are available by using its website's search engine.

Wine to Water

783 W. King St., Suite F
PO Box 2567
Boone, NC 28607
Phone: (828) 355-9655
Website: http://winetowater.org

Wine to Water is a nonprofit organization that is focused on providing clean water to needy people around the world. Its website offers information about the group's projects, video clips of news stories, and a link to a blog that offers frequent updates about the group's work in Haiti and other developing countries.

World Health Organization (WHO)

Avenue Appia 20
1211 Geneva 27
Switzerland
Phone: (41) 22 791 21 11 • fax: (41) 22 791 31 11
Website: www.who.int

The WHO is the directing and coordinating authority for health within the United Nations system. Its website provides separate fact sheets about the various waterborne illnesses, and numerous articles can be accessed through the search engine.

For More Information

Books

Ruth Bjorklund. *Cholera*. Tarrytown, NY: Marshall Cavendish, 2011. Through a number of interesting stories, readers will learn about the history of cholera, its causes, and how dreadful a disease it is for people who suffer from it.

William Caper. *Typhoid Fever: Dirty Food, Dirty Water!* New York: Bearport, 2011. This book introduces readers to typhoid fever by telling the story of a 1906 epidemic in the United States. It also covers what typhoid fever is, how it affects the body, and areas of the world where epidemics are still common.

Dorothy H. Crawford. *Deadly Companions: How Microbes Shaped Our History*. New York: Oxford University Press, 2009. This book uses historical epidemics to explain how microbes and humans have evolved together and the role this has played in the reemergence of new diseases, including those that are waterborne.

Paul Farmer. *Haiti After the Earthquake*. New York: Public-Affairs, 2011. The author is a doctor who gives a firsthand account of the devastation in Haiti after the January 2010 earthquake, which was followed by a massive cholera epidemic that ravaged the country.

Robert D. Morris. *The Blue Death: Disease, Disaster, and the Water We Drink*. New York: HarperCollins, 2007. In this book the author describes waterborne epidemics, credits the scientists who saved millions of lives by discovering waterborne illnesses, and issues a warning about the numerous ways that drinking water is contaminated today.

Periodicals

Rachael Moeller Gorman. "Is Your Tap Water Safe?" *Good Housekeeping*, August 2012. This article tells of an investigation that revealed the presence of numerous pathogens in Americans' drinking water.

Steve Helling and Alex Tresniowski. "Natasha's Choice." *People*, January 17, 2011. The compelling story of Natasha Marcial, a woman who survived the earthquake in Haiti, contracted cholera, and then had to search for her missing children.

Deborah Sontag. "In Haiti, Global Failures on a Cholera Epidemic." *New York Times*, March 31, 2012. This is an eye-opening article about the devastating 2010 cholera epidemic in Haiti and how it began.

Weekly Reader News Edition. "One Year Later: Earthquake Survivors in Haiti Face New Dangers," January 7, 2011. This article explains the many problems that still plagued the people in Haiti a year after the earthquake struck.

Internet Sources

E. Corcoran, C. Nellemann, E. Baker, R. Bos, D. Osborn, and H. Savelli. *Sick Water? The Central Role of Wastewater Management in Sustainable Development*. United Nations Environment Programme and UN-Habitat, 2010. www.unep .org/pdf/SickWater_screen.pdf.

Jennifer Frazer. "Just What Is the Brain-Eating 'Amoeba' *Naegleria Fowleri?*" *The Artful Amoeba* (blog), *Scientific American*, August 17, 2011. http://blogs.scientificamerican .com/artful-amoeba/2011/08/17/just-what-is-the-brain-eating -amoeba-naegleria-fowleri.

Hesperian. *A Community Guide to Environmental Health*, 2012. http://hesperian.org/books-and-resources.

UNICEF. *Children in Pakistan: Six Months After the Floods*, January 2011. www.unicef.org/infobycountry/files/UNICEF _Pakistan_6mos_FINAL-Hires.pdf.

Union of Concerned Scientists. *After the Storm: The Hidden Health Risks of Flooding in a Warning World*, March 2012. www.ucsusa.org/assets/documents/global_warming /climate-change-and-flooding.pdf.

Websites

BrainPOP (www.brainpop.com). This website uses fun interactive activities to educate kids about numerous issues, including water pollution and other issues related to earth's water.

Students for the Environment (www.epa.gov/students). A website especially for young people who are interested in environmental issues such as the importance of keeping water clean and safe for drinking. Features news stories, games, quizzes, and resources for homework.

Water.org (http://water.org). This website explains the important work of the group that was cofounded by actor Matt Damon. It offers facts about the world water crisis and waterborne illness, as well as information about the water-related problems in developing countries such as India, Haiti, and most African nations.

Index

Picture Credits

About the Author

Peggy J. Parks holds a bachelor of science degree from Aquinas College in Grand Rapids, Michigan, where she graduated magna cum laude. An author who has written more than one hundred educational books for children and young adults, Parks lives in Muskegon, Michigan, a town that she says inspires her writing because of its location on the shores of Lake Michigan.